THE OLD
FARMER'S ALMANAC

READERS'
BEST RECIPES

AND THE STORIES BEHIND THEM

12

94 126

The Old Farmer's Almanac Books
PUBLISHER: Sherin Pierce
EDITOR: Janice Stillman
ART DIRECTOR: Colleen Quinnell
FOOD EDITOR: Sarah Perreault
COPY EDITOR: Jack Burnett
EDITORIAL STAFF: Mare-Anne Jarvela, Heidi Stonehill, Tim Clark

V.P., NEW MEDIA AND PRODUCTION: Paul Belliveau
PRODUCTION DIRECTORS: Susan Gross, David Ziarnowski
PRODUCTION ARTISTS: Rachel Kipka, Jennifer Freeman, Janet Grant

DIGITAL EDITOR: Catherine Boeckmann
WEB DESIGNERS: Lou Eastman, Amy O'Brien
E-COMMERCE MANAGER: Alan Henning
PROGRAMMING: Reinvented, Inc.

CONSUMER MARKETING MANAGER: Kate McPherson

COVER AND FOOD PHOTOGRAPHY: Becky Luigart-Stayner
FOOD STYLIST: Ana Kelly
PROP STYLIST: Jan Gautro

For additional information about this and other publications from The Old Farmer's Almanac, visit ALMANAC.COM or call 1-800-ALMANAC.

Distributed in the book trade by Houghton Mifflin Harcourt.

YANKEE PUBLISHING INC., P.O. BOX 520, 1121 MAIN STREET, DUBLIN, NEW HAMPSHIRE 03444

Thank you for buying this cookbook! We hope you enjoy every dish that it inspires. Thanks, too, to everyone who had a hand in it, including printers, distributors, and sales and delivery people.

ISBN/EAN: 978-1-57198-716-7
First Edition

Printed in the United States of America

Readers' Best Recipes
and the stories behind them

How often have you had something to eat and said, "I want that recipe!" (We've all done it!)

Well, say no more: *These* are *those* recipes!

At your fingertips is a collection of recipes from folks all over the United States and Canada. Among them are treasures that have been passed down for generations, the "must make" dishes served at family and holiday gatherings. You've got the crowd-pleasing favorites that people bring to reunions, picnics, and potlucks—the ones that disappear first and leave those who didn't get a taste wishing they'd had one. You also have some original dishes that were "invented" by using ingredients found only in the pantry or fridge to create delicious and much requested suppers. All this, plus a few surprises!

The stories that accompany these recipes give you a glimpse into the cooks' kitchens and a seat at their tables. Their comments are funny, heartwarming, helpful, and true.

Each recipe has been tested and tasted. Comments from our testers and tasters will help you to prepare each dish with confidence and serve it with a smile—and a story.

We hope that you read this book, share the recipes, retell the tales, and perpetuate the traditions. Most of all, we hope that a few of these recipes become *your* favorites, too. Let us know which dishes you like and what you think about the book. We welcome you to our table; please share your comments at **Almanac.com/Feedback**. Enjoy!

—*Almanac editors*

90

208

190

256

40

160

52

168

CONTENTS

BREAKFAST

❧ FRUITED "YOGURT" PARFAIT ❧

To my great surprise, this is delicious even without the fresh fruit! What's more—and better—fully frozen, the "yogurt" (actually the processed cashews) makes a good substitute for ice cream. Beware: Like me, you may have a new addiction! –C.S.

2 cups raw cashews, soaked in water to cover overnight or for 6 to 8 hours, drained

6 tablespoons fresh lemon juice

½ teaspoon sea salt

½ cup ground chia seeds

2 cups blackberries

2 cups blueberries

2 cups raspberries

2 cups sliced strawberries

2 cups sliced nectarines

½ cup date paste (see below)

Combine cashews, lemon juice, sea salt, chia seeds, and 4 cups water in a blender or food processor and process until smooth and creamy. Transfer to covered container and refrigerate until ice cold. (Put into freezer for quicker chill time.) This is the "yogurt."

In a glass jar or bowl with lid, layer "yogurt," fruit, and date paste, alternately. For a sweeter combination, add more date paste with each layer. Top with "yogurt" and cover. Refrigerate for 2 to 4 hours, or until ice cold. Mixture thickens as it chills.

Enjoy this luscious indulgence of rich, creamy, and wholesome goodness. The raw nourishment of nut, seed, and refreshing fruit provides some of the core elements for daily wellness. A great breakfast treat offering vitality throughout the day . . . delicious!

June Taylor, Indian Wells, California

EASY DATE PASTE

Soak six pitted dates in water to cover in a jar until they are very soft (best done the day before). Then, "mash" the dates in the water against the side of the jar with a teaspoon.

❧ CEREAL GRANOLA ❧

I add a bit more oil, honey, and vanilla than the recipe suggests so that the result is moister and chunkier. The mixed berries add color. –C.B.

6 cups old-fashioned oats

1 cup pecan pieces (optional)

¾ cup toasted wheat germ

½ cup brown sugar

½ cup unsweetened flaked coconut

⅓ cup ground flaxseed or whole sesame seeds

½ cup vegetable oil

⅓ cup honey

1½ teaspoons vanilla extract

1 cup dried chopped fruit (cranberries, cherries, apricots, etc.)

Preheat oven to 350°F.

Spread oats in two 10x8-inch pans or one large roasting pan. Bake for 10 minutes, stirring occasionally. Reduce oven to 325°F.

Transfer oats to a bowl. Add pecans (if using), wheat germ, brown sugar, coconut, and ground flaxseed.

In another bowl, combine oil, honey, and vanilla.

Pour oil mixture into oat mixture and stir to coat. Return to baking pans. Bake for 10 minutes. Stir, then bake for 10 minutes more. Remove from oven, add fruit, and lightly stir. Set aside to cool completely. Break into pieces. Store in airtight bags or containers in the refrigerator.

Makes about 8 cups.

This recipe, passed along from my sister Alison, is both healthy and tasty, and all of my guests ask for it! During the holidays, use cranberries and give to friends as a gift.

Beth Fitzgerald, Williamsburg, Ohio

You can buy whole or ground flaxseed in bulk at many health food stores. Grind whole seeds in a coffee grinder and store in an airtight container for several months.

❧ BROWN BUTTER GRANOLA ❧

Two thumbs up! The variety of textures among the seeds, oats, wheat germ, and nuts gives this a fun-in-your-mouth chew, and the cranberries are a wonderful tart counterpoint to the sweetness. Straight out of the bowl or with yogurt for breakfast, it's delish! –D.T.

2 cups old-fashioned oats

½ cup sunflower seeds

½ cup sesame seeds

½ cup dried cranberries or raisins

⅓ cup finely shredded unsweetened coconut

⅓ cup chopped pecans

2 tablespoons chia seeds

⅓ cup butter

½ cup honey

2 tablespoons milk

½ cup wheat germ

Preheat oven to 300°F. Spray a large baking sheet with nonstick cooking spray.

In a bowl, mix together oats, sunflower seeds, sesame seeds, cranberries, coconut, pecans, and chia seeds.

In a saucepan over medium heat, melt butter. Lift pan and swirl several times to ensure even cooking. The butter will begin to foam and deepen in color. Stir constantly. When butter smells nutty and is golden brown, remove from heat. Pour into a glass bowl and stir for 1 minute.

In a separate pan, heat honey and milk to boiling, then set aside to cool. Stir in browned butter. Cool for 1 minute, then pour over oat mixture and stir. Stir in wheat germ.

Spread mixture on prepared baking sheet. Bake for 15 minutes. Stir, then bake for 10 minutes more, or until lightly brown and beginning to crisp. Cool on baking sheet and store in airtight bags or containers.

Makes about 5 cups.

This recipe came from my mother-in-law originally, and I made modifications to it (added the browned butter, chia, and cranberries and switched out another nut for pecans). She passed away more than 6 years ago, so when I make any of her recipes (and I make many), it is very comforting and brings back warm memories, especially for my husband. It is also so special to be able to share "Grandma Jean's" recipes with her grandchildren. She would have loved that!

Terri Gilson, Calgary, Alberta

If honey isn't handy, you can use pure maple syrup for a maple-y flavor.

❧ STUFFED FRENCH TOAST ❧

When I served this to my family for brunch, it was a big hit. The French toast was easier to assemble than I expected. The filling kept the bread slices together, and dipping the three layers of bread in the egg mixture went without a hitch. Baking the French toast in the oven instead of frying it on top of the stove makes a lot of sense; you use less butter and it's less messy. I used one mashed banana in half of the filling and 1 cup sliced fresh strawberries in the other half. Both fillings were very good. –M.A.J.

Filling:

2 packages (8 ounces each) cream cheese, softened

½ cup sour cream or plain yogurt

2 tablespoons sugar

1 teaspoon ground cinnamon

½ teaspoon vanilla extract

2 ripe bananas, mashed, or fresh strawberries, or red raspberry or strawberry preserves

24 slices raisin bread

French toast:

1¼ cups milk

8 eggs

2 tablespoons confectioners' sugar, plus more, if desired

1 teaspoon ground cinnamon

½ teaspoon vanilla extract

warm maple syrup, for serving

Preheat oven to 350°F. Generously grease a 15x10x1-inch baking sheet.

For filling: In a bowl, combine cream cheese, sour cream, sugar, cinnamon, vanilla, and bananas.

Spread filling evenly on one bread slice, then top with another slice. Spread filling evenly on second slice, then top with third slice. Repeat with remaining filling and bread.

For French toast: In a bowl, combine milk, eggs, sugar, cinnamon, and vanilla. Beat until well blended.

Pour egg mixture into a shallow bowl. Dip prepared bread layers into mixture, turning to coat both sides evenly.

Place on prepared baking sheet. Bake for 8 to 10 minutes. Flip and bake for 8 to 10 minutes more, or until golden brown. Dust lightly with additional confectioners' sugar, if desired. Serve with warm maple syrup.

Makes 8 servings.

Almanac favorite

❦ HEALTHY MORNING MUFFINS ❧

1¼ cups all-purpose flour

¾ cup ground flaxseed

½ cup packed brown sugar

½ teaspoon baking soda

½ teaspoon baking powder

½ teaspoon ground nutmeg

½ teaspoon ground cinnamon

½ teaspoon salt

2 large carrots, shredded

1 ripe banana, mashed

2 eggs

⅓ cup milk

2 tablespoons canola oil

2 tablespoons peanut butter

½ cup pecan pieces

Preheat oven to 375°F. Grease a 12-cup muffin tin or line with papers.

In a bowl, combine flour, flaxseed meal, brown sugar, baking soda, baking powder, nutmeg, cinnamon, and salt. Mix well.

In another bowl, combine carrots, banana, eggs, milk, oil, and peanut butter. Add flour mixture and pecan pieces. Stir just until combined. Do not overmix.

Fill muffin tins two-thirds full. Bake for 15 minutes, or until a toothpick inserted into the center comes out clean.

Makes 12 muffins.

I made this up because I love to have muffins first thing in the morning or available for an easy snack, but I don't love how much sugar many muffins contain. This recipe has protein and fiber and just the right amount of sweetness. I especially enjoy putting these muffins in my toaster oven the day after they are baked, then spreading peanut butter on them. Yum!

Marisol Maddox, Big Indian, New York

The word "muffin" likely comes from an Old German word, *muffe,* meaning a small cake.

BREAKFAST

❧ GRANMA'S EGG ❧ AND SHREDDED WHEAT

TESTER'S COMMENTS

This makes a quick, easy, and comforting breakfast. For kids (of all ages), the process, the shredded wheat, and the mushing up make eating playful. –H.S.

1 or 2 large shredded wheat biscuits
1 to 3 tablespoons butter or margarine, divided
1 or 2 eggs (1 per biscuit)
salt and freshly ground black pepper, to taste

Place shredded wheat in a bowl. Bring a pot of water to a boil.

Melt 1 to 2 tablespoons butter in a skillet over medium heat and fry egg to "over easy," or until white is firm but yolk is runny.

After turning egg, pour boiling water over shredded wheat. Immediately drain water off into sink (use spatula to hold shredded wheat). Place 1 tablespoon butter on each shredded wheat biscuit. Top with fried egg. Season with salt and pepper. Mush egg yolk into shredded wheat and serve.

Makes 1 to 2 servings.

My grandmother used to feed this to my father when he was a boy. He loves it to this day. I remember the first time she cooked it for me. I thought it was odd, but then I tasted it and was sold for good! This is a great alternative to eggs and toast! Even my picky husband and kids love it. Try it—you'll love it too!

Anonymous

❧ CREAMY SHREDDED ❧ POTATOES

TESTER'S COMMENTS

Think of a potato omelet served in squares . . . that's this! The top is crisp and crunchy, the bottom nicely chewy. For best results, make enough egg mixture to almost cover the potatoes in the baking dish. –D.T.

5 medium russet potatoes
⅓ cup butter, melted
½ cup chopped onion
1 can (5 ounces) evaporated milk

3 eggs, beaten
1¼ teaspoons salt
⅛ teaspoon freshly ground black pepper
1 cup shredded cheddar cheese, divided

Preheat oven to 350°F. Grease an 8x8-inch baking dish.

Peel potatoes and place in a bowl of cold water to prevent discoloration. Set aside.

Melt butter in a skillet over medium heat. Add onions and sauté for 5 minutes, or until limp. Add milk and bring to a boil. Remove from heat.

Shred potatoes by hand or in a food processor.

In a bowl, combine eggs, salt, and pepper. Beat until frothy. Add shredded potatoes. Stir to combine. Add milk mixture. Add ¾ cup of cheese to potato mixture and mix well.

Pour into prepared baking dish. Bake for 1 hour, or until egg mixture firms up. Top with remaining cheese and bake for 5 to 10 minutes more, or until cheese melts. Cut into squares and serve hot.

Makes 4 to 6 servings.

Almanac favorite

Turnip Soufflé

Pass warm maple syrup alongside the soufflé to complement its delicate flavor or increase the spices to suit your taste (adding only a bit at a time is best). –S.L.P.

¼ cup (½ stick) unsalted butter,
   plus extra for greasing ramekins

1 pound turnips, peeled and cut into chunks

½ cup heavy cream

1 bay leaf

2 whole cloves

pinch of freshly grated nutmeg

3 tablespoons all-purpose flour

pinch of kosher or sea salt

pinch of white pepper (optional)

4 large eggs, separated

Preheat oven to 375°F. Butter six ramekin dishes.

Bring a pot of salted water to a boil and add turnips. Cook for 20 minutes, or until tender. Drain and pat dry. Press through food mill or ricer. Set aside.

In a saucepan over medium heat, combine cream, bay leaf, cloves, and nutmeg. When cream is scalded, strain it and discard solids.

In another saucepan over medium heat, melt butter. Whisk in flour and cook for 1 minute. (Do not brown mixture.) Whisk in strained cream, half at a time. Whisk in turnips. Cook, stirring constantly, until mixture thickens. Season with salt and white pepper (if using). Cool to room temperature.

In a bowl, beat egg yolks. Fold in one-third of turnip mixture. Fold in remaining turnip mixture.

In a chilled bowl, beat egg whites until stiff. Fold egg whites into turnip mixture.

Spoon mixture into prepared dishes and place on a baking sheet. Bake for 18 to 20 minutes, or until soufflés are browned and rise 1 inch or more.

Makes 6 servings.

Almanac favorite

BREAKFAST

APPETIZERS

ℰ Black Bean Salsa ℐ

Six people ate all of this in one sitting. While it's very good as is, for sharper flavor, increase the spices and/or add chopped cilantro or green onions. –D.T.

1 can (15 ounces) black beans, drained and rinsed

1 can (15.25 ounces) whole corn, drained and rinsed

2 medium tomatoes, diced

1 red bell pepper, diced

1 green bell pepper, diced

½ cup diced red onion

1 can (4 ounces) chopped green chiles, drained

¼ cup lime juice

½ teaspoon salt

½ teaspoon ground cumin

½ teaspoon cayenne pepper

⅓ cup olive oil

⅓ cup red-wine vinegar

dash of hot sauce

In a bowl, combine beans, corn, tomatoes, peppers, onions, and chiles.

In another bowl or jar with lid, mix lime juice, salt, cumin, cayenne, olive oil, vinegar, and hot sauce. Add to bean mixture. Stir, cover, and let sit in refrigerator overnight before serving. Serve with tortilla chips.

Makes 8 to 10 servings.

Years ago, a friend fixed this for a potluck. I make it every time we have a casual gathering. It can be served as a salad, too!

Margaret Hill, Louisville, Kentucky

To get more juice out of a lime or lemon, put it in the microwave for 15 to 20 seconds before juicing.

JALAPEÑO POPPER SPREAD

Perfect for a party, this is quick to make, tasty, and addictive! –D.T.

2 packages (8 ounces each) cream cheese, softened
1 jar (12 ounces) diced jalapeños, with juice
2 cans (4 ounces each) chopped green chiles, with juice
1 cup mayonnaise
1 cup grated Parmesan cheese

In a microwave-safe casserole, combine cream cheese, jalapeños (I use almost all of them), chiles, mayonnaise, and Parmesan. Heat in the microwave until piping hot.

Makes 10 to 12 servings.

You can serve this with tortilla chips, crackers, or bread. It is awesome!
Sharon Whisler, Fremont, Nebraska

FRESH MEXICAN SALSA

This salsa is juicy and chunky and has a nice, fresh "kick" to it—the way salsa should be! It's well worth the time it takes to chop all the veggies. –S.P.

1½ cups peeled and diced juicy tomatoes or 1 can (14 ounces) diced tomatoes, drained
1 can (10 ounces) diced tomatoes with green chiles
3 green onions, diced
2 chile peppers (such as serrano or jalapeño), seeded and diced
1 bell pepper, diced
½ onion, diced
¼ cup chopped fresh cilantro
2 tablespoons fresh lemon juice
1 teaspoon sugar or more, to taste
½ teaspoon lemon zest
salt and freshly ground black pepper, to taste

In a bowl, combine tomatoes, tomatoes with chiles, green onions, chiles, bell peppers, onions, cilantro, lemon juice, sugar, lemon zest, and salt and pepper. Add more chile peppers, cilantro, lemon juice, salt, or pepper, as desired. Cover and keep refrigerated. Use within a week and a half.

To use up toward end of freshness, preheat oven to 350°F. Mix remaining salsa with spicy mustard and honey, to taste. Pour over chicken breasts in a casserole. Add enough water to keep chicken breasts from sticking to pan. Bake for 30 minutes.

Makes 1 quart.

My daughter, Cara, moved to Tokyo, Japan, several years ago. She loves Mexican food! On her budget, she can not find what she likes there, so she has continued to experiment to make her own Mexican dishes. This is her salsa that she uses for parties with chips, on enchiladas and burritos, on scrambled eggs for breakfast, and to give to friends. I love it, too, and make it throughout the summer!
Donna Phillips, Winchester, Virginia

SPICY SWEET BACON CHICKEN TENDERS

These are firehouse hot with the recommended 2 tablespoons chipotle chili powder, yet tasters extinguished them in seconds. When buying chicken, note that true chicken tenders can be skimpy. For more substantial pieces, consider getting boneless, skinless breasts and cutting them into strips. You don't want the chicken pieces to be done before the bacon has cooked. –C.S.

8 thick slices bacon

8 boneless, skinless chicken breast tenders

½ cup brown sugar

2 tablespoons chipotle chili powder

Preheat oven to 350°F.

Wrap a bacon slice around each chicken tender. Secure top and bottom of bacon with two toothpicks per tender.

In a shallow bowl, mix together brown sugar and chipotle chili powder. Roll bacon-wrapped chicken in mixture, then place on rimmed baking sheet. Bake for 35 minutes, or until chicken is fully cooked and bacon is crisp. (Place under broiler, if bacon is not crispy.) Cool briefly on baking sheet, then roll in drippings and serve.

Makes 8 servings.

This recipe was handed down to me by my sister-in-law. I was skeptical at first, but everyone loves these! I make them all the time for my guests and at family gatherings.

Nancy Parkinson, Hull, Massachusetts

Chipotle chili powder is made from dried, smoked jalapeños.
Chili powder is made from dried chiles and other spices.

APPETIZERS

ℰ CHEESE ON TOAST ℈

TESTER'S COMMENTS

There is nothing but good things to say about this! It tastes rich and indulgent. Using Gouda cheese, it turned out thick and creamy. Fresh corn would have been ideal, but I tried this in March, so I used frozen. Canned corn, drained, would have been fine, too. I could eat this every day. –D.T.

2 tablespoons (¼ stick) butter

1 small onion, finely diced

1 teaspoon kosher or sea salt

½ cup milk

½ pound shredded cheese, such as aged Gouda or cheddar

2 egg yolks, beaten

2 cups fresh corn kernels

2 teaspoons minced fresh parsley, savory, or other herb, plus more for garnish

6 slices sourdough or other crusty bread, toasted

Melt butter in a skillet over medium heat. Add onions and salt and cook for 6 minutes, or until onions are translucent. Add milk and stir for 5 minutes, or until slightly thickened. Reduce heat to the lowest setting and sprinkle in cheese, stirring continuously. When fully melted, slowly pour ¼ cup of mixture into a bowl with egg yolks, whisking quickly. Whisk in ¼ cup more, then pour back into skillet. Stir until thickened. Add corn and parsley and mix well. Serve hot over toast, garnished with fresh herbs.

Makes 6 servings as an appetizer, 3 as a main course.

Legend has it that this recipe came from Mildred B. Larrabee, a Yankee *magazine reader who shared it for publication in a 1966 edition, along with the story of an ill-fated ship from Amsterdam that foundered in a storm off the coast of Maine in December 1710. On board were hundreds of wheels of wax-coated cheese, many of which floated safely to shore on Peaks Island. (The crew was not so lucky.) "The women [on the island] were hard-taxed to find ways in which to utilize it in such ingenious recipes as to avoid the exclamation: 'Oh, not cheese again!'" This, a variation on Welsh rarebit, was one of their inventions.*

Almanac favorite

❧ FLUFFY CORN FRITTERS ❧

These fritters absorb quite a bit of oil while cooking, so have extra close by. It will be worth it: They are light and crispy straight from the pan. My first bite crunched in the best way and then melted in my mouth. –S.L.P.

½ cup vegetable oil, divided

4 eggs, separated

2 cups canned cream-style corn

2 tablespoons butter or margarine, melted

¾ teaspoon salt

1 cup cracker crumbs

1 teaspoon baking powder

Heat 3 tablespoons oil in a skillet over medium heat.

In a bowl, beat egg whites until stiff.

In another bowl, beat yolks slightly. Add corn, butter, and salt.

In a separate bowl, combine cracker crumbs and baking powder, then add to corn mixture. Fold in egg whites.

Drop by spoonfuls into hot oil and cook for 1 to 2 minutes per side, or until golden brown. Add more oil to pan as needed.

Makes about 40 fritters.

Generally speaking, canned corn is a drag. But good fresh corn is available for such a short time each year. What's a corn lover to do? Here's one good answer.

Almanac favorite

Even the tiniest bit of egg yolk in separated egg whites
can affect their leavening ability. To remove, touch the yolk with a cloth
moistened in cold water—it will cling to the cloth like a magnet.

❧ Hummus ❧

Hummus is easy to make. Use as a dip with raw vegetables or spread on bread or crackers. –J.S.

1 can (20 ounces) chickpeas or 2½ cups
  cooked chickpeas

¼ cup fresh lemon juice

2 cloves garlic, minced

2 tablespoons olive oil, divided

¼ cup tahini

salt and freshly ground black pepper, to taste

fresh minced parsley, for garnish

Drain chickpeas and reserve liquid.

In a blender or food processor, combine chickpeas, lemon juice, garlic, 1 tablespoon olive oil, and tahini. Blend until smooth. Add enough reserved liquid to achieve creamy consistency. Taste and add salt and pepper. Transfer to bowl, drizzle with remaining olive oil, and garnish with parsley. Refrigerate until ready to serve.

Makes about 2 cups.

Almanac favorite

❧ Southwestern Pumpkin Hummus ❧

I thought I'd tried every kind of hummus out there—and then came along pumpkin hummus. The garlic gives it a nice kick, and the crunch of the pumpkin seeds is a nice finishing touch. –S.L.P.

8 cloves garlic

¼ cup fresh cilantro

¼ cup lime juice

¼ cup tahini

2 tablespoons pumpkin
  oil or olive oil

1 can (15-ounces)
  pumpkin purée

3 teaspoons cumin

1 teaspoon salt

½ teaspoon chili powder

½ teaspoon chipotle
  pepper (ground or flakes)

pumpkin seeds, for garnish

Combine all of the ingredients (except garnish) in a food processor and blend until smooth. Transfer to a bowl and cover. Refrigerate overnight. Garnish with pumpkin seeds and drizzle with extra oil before serving. Serve with vegetables, crackers, or tortilla chips.

Makes about 2 cups.

Second-prize winner in *The 2010 Old Farmer's Almanac* Reader Recipe Contest for pumpkin
Sharon Ricci, Mendon, New York

MY MOM'S PICKLED SHRIMP

This is an excellent recipe with delicious results. The shrimp brighten your mouth with a hint of pickle. –C.S.

1 cup white-wine vinegar

½ cup olive oil

1 large onion, sliced into half-rings

2 tablespoons pickling spice

1 teaspoon salt, or to taste

2 pounds raw shrimp, peeled, deveined, and tails removed

In a stockpot, combine vinegar, olive oil, onions, pickling spice, salt, and 3 cups water. Bring to a rolling boil. Add shrimp and boil for 5 minutes. Remove from heat and cool to room temperature.

Refrigerate overnight.

Lift shrimp and onions with slotted spoon and transfer to serving dish. Serve cold.

Makes 12 servings.

My mother used to make this every Christmas for us to nibble on while we waited for dinner. Everyone looked forward to it as a staple of the holiday.

Hugh Rardin, Kitty Hawk, North Carolina

If using frozen shrimp, defrost them before cooking by placing them in a colander under cold running water for about 5 minutes.

✄ SHRIMP DIP ✄

TESTER'S COMMENTS

Simply delicious. Mix all of the ingredients in a bowl, chill the dip for a few hours (or overnight), and serve. Instead of finely chopping all of the shrimp, I left a few bigger chunks for texture. –M.A.J.

- 2 pounds freshly boiled shrimp, peeled, deveined, and finely chopped
- 2 packages (8 ounces each) cream cheese, softened
- 1 cup mayonnaise
- 2 tablespoons chili sauce
- 1 tablespoon Worcestershire sauce
- 1 medium yellow onion, finely grated
- juice of 1 to 2 lemons, to taste
- salt and freshly ground black pepper, to taste

In a glass bowl, mix together shrimp, cream cheese, mayonnaise, chili sauce, Worcestershire sauce, onions, lemon juice, and salt and pepper. Refrigerate for 1 to 2 hours before serving.

Makes 3½ to 4 cups, depending on shrimp size.

My sister-in-law gave me this recipe about 35 years ago. It was so delicious that I had to have it. I adjusted the original recipe to my liking. I make it for every family event. It is so good, some just get a bowl and eat it by itself! Good to dip with vegetables fresh from your garden or your favorite chip. A very simple recipe that should only take 30 to 40 minutes to complete.

Cindy Walker, Mobile, Alabama

In the grocery store, chili sauce is usually found near the ketchup.

CRAB DIP

Lump crab is expensive; just get the best quality that you can afford. The higher-quality the crab, the better the result. –L.R.

2 packages (8 ounces each) cream cheese, softened
1 cup sour cream
½ cup grated Parmesan cheese
3 tablespoons mayonnaise
½ teaspoon ground mustard
¼ teaspoon Old Bay seasoning
juice of 1 lemon
2 to 3 drops onion juice
2 to 3 drops Worcestershire sauce
1 pound lump crabmeat
paprika

Preheat oven to 325°F. Grease a 9x9-inch casserole.

In a bowl, mix together cream cheese, sour cream, Parmesan, mayonnaise, mustard, Old Bay, lemon juice, onion juice, and Worcestershire sauce. Stir in crabmeat. Sprinkle with paprika. Transfer to prepared casserole. Bake for 35 minutes, or until bubbly.

Makes 12 servings.

I learned how to make this recipe from my college roommate in the early 1980s. Her parents used to make it and now, 30 years later, it's still a delicious showstopper.

Tarver Harris, Stafford, Virginia

The four basic grades of crabmeat are jumbo lump,
lump or backfin, special, and claw.

ROCKFISH DIP

Rockfish are difficult to get in our corner of New England, so I used haddock, and I wouldn't hesitate to use cod. Old Bay seasoning brings a lot to the dish, so don't skimp; I used 1 tablespoon and would use more next time. Nonetheless, when I took this dip to a get-together, the numerous tasters gave it rave reviews. –C.S.

½ to 1 whole yellow or sweet onion, diced

½ cup diced red or green bell pepper

2 to 3 tablespoons butter

1 package (8 ounces) cream cheese, softened

¼ cup mayonnaise

¼ cup sour cream

Old Bay seasoning, to taste (or make your own, see below)

freshly ground black pepper, to taste

1 pound rockfish (such as Atlantic striped bass; see Tester's Comments above), poached and chopped or shredded

½ cup shredded Monterey Jack cheese

½ cup shredded cheddar cheese

grated Parmesan cheese, for topping

Preheat oven to 350°F. Grease a shallow baking dish.

In a skillet, sauté onions and bell peppers in butter until soft. Set aside.

In a bowl, mix together cream cheese, mayonnaise, and sour cream until smooth. Stir in Old Bay and pepper. Add fish, sautéed onions and peppers, Monterey Jack, and cheddar.

Transfer to prepared dish. Bake for 8 to 12 minutes. Sprinkle with Parmesan and bake for 5 minutes more, or until mixture is bubbling and Parmesan melts. Serve with crackers, tortilla chips, or sliced baguette.

Makes 8 to 12 servings.

My husband and I love to fish for Atlantic stripers in the Chesapeake Bay. This recipe is perfect for using extra fish!

Debra Goodier, Gloucester, Virginia

HOW TO MAKE SEAFOOD SEASONING

In a bowl, combine . . .

2 tablespoons bay leaf powder

2 tablespoons celery salt

1 tablespoon ground mustard

2 teaspoons freshly ground black pepper

2 teaspoons ground ginger

2 teaspoons sweet or smoked paprika

1 teaspoon ground allspice

1 teaspoon ground cloves

1 teaspoon ground nutmeg

1 teaspoon ground white pepper

½ teaspoon ground cardamom

½ teaspoon ground mace

½ teaspoon crushed red pepper flakes

¼ teaspoon ground cinnamon

Store in an airtight container.

✎ DRESSED-UP CRAB RANGOON DIP ✎

TESTER'S COMMENTS

If you like Crab Rangoon, you will like this dip. In fact, I now prefer this dip to the Chinese menu appetizer! –S.L.P.

12 ounces cream cheese, softened

2 cans (6 ounces each) crabmeat, well-drained and picked over for shells

3 scallions, chopped

2 tablespoons chopped sweet roasted red peppers

¾ cup shredded Swiss cheese

⅓ cup grated Parmesan cheese

1 teaspoon prepared horseradish

1 tablespoon Worcestershire sauce

1 tablespoon milk

¼ teaspoon garlic powder

¼ teaspoon salt

⅛ teaspoon freshly ground black pepper

2 tablespoons chopped slivered almonds

1 scallion, green part only, chopped, for garnish

Preheat oven to 375°F. Grease an 8x8-inch baking dish.

In a bowl, mix together cream cheese, crabmeat, scallions, roasted peppers, Swiss cheese, Parmesan, horseradish, Worcestershire sauce, milk, garlic powder, salt, and pepper.

Transfer mixture to prepared baking dish. Bake for 20 to 25 minutes, or until bubbly around edges. Top with almonds and bake for 5 minutes more.

Garnish with chopped green scallions.

Makes 25 servings.

Third-prize winner in *The 2015 Old Farmer's Almanac* Reader Recipe Contest for dips and spreads
Debbie Reid, Clearwater, Florida

The "horse" in horseradish may refer to the large size
of the plant root or the strength of its flavor.
One teaspoon of horseradish contains only 2 calories.

APPETIZERS

❧ ONION AND CHIVE PANEER CHEESE SPREAD ❧

The paneer that I've had in Indian restaurants is usually firm and slightly "squeaky"; this version, made with whole pasteurized cow's milk, is utterly different. While still warm, it was light and fluffy and so delicious. Later, chilled and firmer, the flavors had mellowed and blended together. In the morning, with spinach in an omelet, it was heavenly. I highly recommend giving this a try. It's much (much!) easier than it may appear; 90 percent of the time is spent waiting for the milk to boil. Plus, making cheese spread will impress friends and family! –D.T.

1 gallon whole milk (I use fresh, unpasteurized goat milk)

½ cup distilled white vinegar

3 tablespoons butter, softened

1 tablespoon chopped fresh or freeze-dried chives

1 teaspoon garlic powder

1 teaspoon onion powder

1 teaspoon dried minced onions

1 teaspoon salt

Pour milk into 2-gallon pot. Heat over medium-low for 45 to 60 minutes, or just until milk begins to boil. Stir frequently so that it does not stick and scorch. Remove from heat. Stir in vinegar. Set aside for 15 minutes to separate curds from whey.

Cover separate pot or bowl with cheesecloth or flour sack. Carefully pour hot curds and whey through cheesecloth into pot. Pull up cheesecloth corners and drain out most of whey. Return curds (contents of cheesecloth) to 2-gallon pot.

Add butter, chives, garlic powder, onion powder, dried onions, and salt to pot and stir. Add enough hot whey, a little at a time, to help butter to melt and dried spices to blend evenly. Stir until mixture gathers into a ball.

Cover another bowl with cheesecloth. Lay cheese ball in cheesecloth. Gather cheesecloth corners and twist top to squeeze out more liquid into bowl. Let cheese hang for a few minutes (if using raw, unpasteurized milk, do not leave out of fridge for too long). Transfer to a resealable plastic bag or covered container and refrigerate for a few hours to allow onions and chives to soften.

Serve cold, spread on crackers, or warm, with sautéed spinach on herbed flat bread. Pour remaining whey in garden for fertilizer.

Makes 3 cups.

I started raising dairy goats a few years ago. I have four goats that I milk every day. I had an abundant supply of milk that I was afraid would spoil before my family could drink it all. I found an easy recipe for making Indian paneer cheese and modified it to make a spread using fresh, unpasteurized goat milk to eat on crackers. Traditional paneer cheese is very similar to firm tofu and can be cut into cubes and added to vegetarian dishes to provide protein, but I really like spreading it on crackers, so I softened it up by leaving some of the whey in it and made it a little creamier by adding butter. My goat milk does not have much cream in it. My family and friends really rave about it—even the ones who won't even try drinking my fresh goat milk.

Rebecca Wilson, Tellico Plains, Tennessee

Mom's Gorton Spread

2 to 3 pounds pork butt or blade

2 to 3 medium onions, divided

1 teaspoon salt, or to taste

¼ to ½ teaspoon freshly ground black pepper,
  or to taste

2 to 3 teaspoons ground allspice, or to taste

1 to 2 teaspoons ground cloves, or to taste

Cut pork into large chunks and place in a large pot. Cover with water. Chop one onion and add to pot. Stir in salt and pepper. Cook over medium heat for 1 to 2 hours, or until pork is cooked through. Remove pork and set aside to cool. Reserve cooking liquid. Skim off any fat.

Grind pork with cooked onions and add 1 to 2 raw onions. Return pork to reserved cooking liquid. Add allspice and cloves. Taste and add more salt and pepper, if desired. Cook over medium heat for about 1 hour, or until all liquid evaporates. Taste periodically for seasonings and adjust to taste. Serve on toast or crackers or as sandwich filling.

Makes about 6 cups.

This dish (sometimes called cretons*) is of French-Canadian origin, and countless cooks have added their own special touches to the recipe. This is my mother's and the best I've ever tasted. Some of the measurements are guessed, but the ingredients stay the same. The measurements were never written down. It's a case of trial and error. Everything is "to taste"!*

Anonymous

Gorton can also be made with ground pork,
saving you the work of grinding the pork and other
ingredients yourself—and it tastes just as good.

❦ FLORENTINE SPINACH DIP ❧

Tasters were soon addicted to this warm, cheesy dip. One even asked to lick the emptied casserole! –S.L.P.

2 packages (8 ounces each) cream cheese, softened

1 cup Alfredo sauce (see recipe, page 51)

1 box (10 ounces) frozen spinach, thawed and squeezed dry

½ cup chopped artichoke hearts

¼ cup diced sun-dried tomatoes

¼ cup diced sweet roasted red peppers

2 cups shredded Italian cheese blend

½ cup grated Parmesan cheese

¼ teaspoon Italian seasoning

1 dash hot sauce

Preheat oven to 350°F. Grease a 2-quart casserole.

In a bowl, mix together cream cheese, Alfredo sauce, spinach, artichoke hearts, tomatoes, roasted peppers, cheeses, Italian seasoning, and hot sauce until combined. Transfer to prepared casserole. Bake for 25 to 30 minutes, or until golden brown.

Makes 25 servings.

First-prize winner in *The 2015 Old Farmer's Almanac* Reader Recipe Contest for dips and spreads
Crystal Schlueter, Northglenn, Colorado

HOW TO ROAST PEPPERS

Preheat the broiler. Cut peppers in half and remove the core and seeds.
Lay peppers on a broiler rack or baking sheet, cut side down,
and place under the heat until the skin is blackened. Transfer hot peppers
to a brown paper bag, close the top tightly, and let them steam
for 10 minutes. Remove from the bag and peel off the
charred skin. Store in a jar in the refrigerator.

APPETIZERS

❧ MINIATURE RICE AND CHEESE BALLS ❧

Served warm (freshly cooked or reheated), these little nuggets melt in your mouth. Feel free to exchange a couple of ingredients: a different cheese (perhaps a pepper jack cheese or a Havarti with dill), rice, or bread crumbs (I used seasoned whole wheat). Make sure that the mixture chills well before cooking; it forms balls best when good and cold. –M.A.J.

1 tablespoon shortening

1 tablespoon all-purpose flour

½ teaspoon salt

½ cup whole milk

1 cup shredded sharp cheddar cheese

2 cups cooked white rice

2 eggs, beaten

seasoned fine bread crumbs

vegetable oil for frying, about 2 inches deep

Melt shortening in a saucepan over medium heat. Add flour and salt and stir. Add milk and stir to incorporate. Cook until thickened, stirring. Add cheddar and cook until it melts. Add cooked rice and mix well.

Transfer to a container, cover, and chill overnight, or for at least 12 hours.

To assemble: Put eggs into a shallow bowl.

Spread bread crumbs on a plate.

Shape chilled rice mixture into balls (at least walnut-size). Dip each ball into egg mixture, then roll in bread crumbs.

Heat oil in a skillet to 375°F, or until hot enough to fry. (To test oil temperature, drop a small bread cube into oil; it should sizzle, or fry, evenly.) Carefully put a few rice balls into oil and cook for 2 to 3 minutes. Turn them over and cook until golden brown all around. Watch carefully; balls can break while cooking.

Makes 10 to 20 balls, depending on size.

These miniature rice and cheese balls have been a family tradition for many years. They are always served with Easter dinner and complement ham very well. Crispiness on the outside with creamy cheese and rice on the inside make this a special treat. Everyone in our family looks forward to these little nuggets each year. My mother-in-law needs to double or triple the recipe just to keep up with the demand.

Betty Gair, Allentown, Pennsylvania

APPETIZERS

PEPPERY PECANS

As a party snack, nothing could be easier to make. Even the nuts get in a festive mood: They make little popping sounds for several minutes after coming out of the oven. –H.S.

⅓ cup melted butter

1 tablespoon Worcestershire sauce

1 teaspoon cayenne pepper

1 teaspoon freshly ground black pepper

1 teaspoon salt

4 cups pecans

Preheat oven to 300°F.

In a bowl, combine melted butter, Worcestershire sauce, cayenne, black pepper, and salt and mix well. Add pecans and stir until well coated.

Spread coated pecans on a baking sheet with a rim. Bake for 15 to 20 minutes, stirring every 5 minutes. Remove from oven and cool before serving. Store in an airtight container.

Makes 4 cups.

I saw a recipe in a newspaper, then tweaked it to suit my family. I love to make this to snack on anytime and have made it to serve with cake and punch for showers or other parties.

Nelda McMillan, Nashville, Arkansas

Keep a cold beverage at hand when you eat these—they have a spicy
kick that gets to you a few seconds after swallowing.

❦ PESTO STRATA ❧

A loaf casserole, instead of a round dish, gives this a nice shape that displays the layers. If a loaf dish is not available, don't despair: One taste, and people will not even notice the shape. –J.S.

Pesto:

2 cups fresh Italian parsley without stems

¾ cup Parmesan cheese

1 clove garlic

3 tablespoons olive oil

1 slice bread

½ teaspoon salt

¼ teaspoon freshly ground black pepper

Filling:

2 packages (8 ounces each) cream cheese, softened

½ cup (1 stick) unsalted butter, softened

For pesto: In a food processor or blender, combine parsley, Parmesan, garlic, olive oil, bread, salt, and pepper and process until smooth. Add additional oil as necessary to create a smooth paste.

For filling: In a bowl, mix together cream cheese and butter. Set aside.

To assemble: Line a deep bowl or container with plastic wrap. Put one-third of filling on bottom, followed by one-third of pesto. Repeat layers two more times.

Cover and place in refrigerator. When ready to serve, invert onto serving dish and remove plastic wrap.

Makes 10 to 12 servings.

Second-prize winner in *The 2015 Old Farmer's Almanac* Reader Recipe Contest for dips and spreads
Nancy Vargas, Sierra Madre, California

Parsley comes in curly and Italian types. They can be
used interchangeably in recipes, although some cooks prefer
the slightly sweeter taste of Italian parsley.

APPETIZERS

❧ RED BEET EGGS ☙

These are really good and really pretty! When you slice them in half, there's the bright yellow yolk in the center and bright pink bleeding into the firm egg white. The sweet/sour from the marinade is delicious with the egg—a good alternative to deviled eggs any time of year. –D.T.

1 cup apple cider vinegar

1 cup sugar

1 can (15 ounces) beets, whole, cut, or sliced, with juice

6 hard-boiled eggs, cooled and peeled

In a bowl, combine vinegar, sugar, and 1 cup water. Stir until sugar is dissolved. Carefully add beets, with juice. Add eggs, making sure that each egg is immersed in the mixture. Cover and refrigerate overnight. Eggs will be ready to eat the next day.

Six more eggs may be added to same beet mixture when first six have been eaten.

Makes 6 servings.

This is my grandmother's way of making red beet eggs. Everyone has a different way. This is one of the Pennsylvania Dutch "Seven Sweets and Seven Sours." I like this because it's simple and easy to remember, and the sweet and sour is in perfect balance. So good.

Celeste Brooks, East Petersburg, Pennsylvania

To remove beet stains from your fingers, rub them briskly
with salt and then wash with soap and cool water.

APPETIZERS

MILANESE MUSHROOMS

TESTER'S COMMENTS

Here's a great option when you need something quick, easy, and mild enough for even picky palates. To perk them up a bit, add your favorite chopped herb. The cottage cheese and lack of bread crumbs keep them light. –C.S.

1 pound whole fresh mushrooms

melted butter

1 package (10 ounces) frozen chopped spinach, thawed and squeezed dry

1 cup cottage cheese

1 clove garlic, finely minced

1 teaspoon freshly ground black pepper

⅓ cup grated Parmesan cheese

Preheat oven to 400°F.

Remove stems from mushrooms and mince. (Leave mushroom caps whole.) Brush top of caps with melted butter. Brush inside of caps, if desired.

In a bowl, combine spinach, cottage cheese, garlic, minced mushroom stems, and pepper and mix thoroughly. Spoon mixture into buttered caps. Top with Parmesan. Bake for 10 minutes. Serve warm.

Makes about 36 stuffed mushrooms, depending on size.

My mom made this recipe for as long as I can remember. I'd be sitting next to her, both of us stuffing mushroom caps, talking about anything and everything. I'd put as much Parmesan on each as she'd let me get away with. Then we'd just chitchat while we cleaned up and waited for them to be done. I miss my mom dearly, but I truly feel her presence with me every time I make this recipe.

Lucia Whitten, Huntington Beach, California

One 10-ounce package of frozen spinach equals
about 1½ pounds of fresh spinach.

❦ STUFFED GRAPE LEAVES ❧

Grape leaves come in different sizes and in different-size jars. With the stovetop method, I prepared two-thirds of the recipe, using a 1 pound jar of leaves for 2 pounds of ground meat (1 pound each of lamb and a beef/pork/veal mix). I had plenty. Instead of tomato sauce, I used two 12-ounce cans of diced tomatoes with basil and oregano. This recipe is easier to make than it might appear, and everyone enjoyed them! –M.A.J.

Filling:

2 tablespoons light olive oil or vegetable oil

½ onion, minced

minced garlic, to taste

seasonings, to taste, or ½ teaspoon freshly ground black pepper and 1 tablespoon herbes de Provence, crushed

2 cups cooked rice

2 to 3 pounds ground meat (pork, lamb, or beef; chicken and turkey are not recommended)

2 jars prepared grape leaves (see Tester's Comments for jar sizes)

1 can (28 ounces) tomato sauce or 3 cans (12 ounces each) diced tomatoes

1 cup chicken or vegetable broth

For filling: Heat olive oil in a skillet until shimmering. Add onions and cook until soft. Stir in garlic and seasonings. Remove from heat after garlic softens. Transfer to a bowl. Fold in rice until evenly mixed; avoid mushing rice grains.
Add ground meat. Gently mix until evenly blended. Avoid compacting mixture, or meat may become tough and will not absorb flavor from leaves and sauce.

To assemble: Rinse and drain grape leaves. Pat dry with paper towel, if desired. Lay down one whole leaf, vein side up, and trim off stem. Place ¾ teaspoon to 2 tablespoons filling just above place where stem met leaf. (Amount depends on size of leaf.) Fold up bottom of leaf to cover filling, fold in sides of leaf, and roll up to enclose filling. Rolling should be firm enough to be tidy, but not tight; filling will expand a bit and

leaf may tear in cooking. (If a leaf tears, patch with piece of another leaf.) Set rolled leaf on a platter or baking sheet, with seam of leaf on bottom to keep it from loosening. Repeat with remaining leaves. (Roll extra filling into balls and freeze for another meal.)

To cook on stovetop: Line bottom and (roughly) sides of large pan or Dutch oven with parchment paper to avoid scorching or keep heat low.

Spread ½ cup of tomato sauce in pan. Add rolled leaves in single layer, close but not snug. Top with more sauce. Repeat layers, placing the rolls in each layer perpendicular to those below (to avoid their becoming compacted and tough). Lay extra grape leaves atop rolls and cover with sauce and broth. Heat slowly, on medium, to bring to low simmer. Cover and cook for 20 minutes, or until filling is cooked through.

To cook in oven: Preheat oven to 375°F. Omit parchment paper. Layer sauce and rolls, as directed for stovetop. If Dutch oven has a tight-fitting lid, reduce final broth portion to ½ cup. Bake for 1 hour, or until filling is cooked through.

To cook in slow cooker: Layer sauce and rolls, as directed, and omit broth. Cook on low for 4 to 6 hours.

To make ahead: Prepare rolls and layer in pan with sauce. Cover and refrigerate immediately. Cook within 2 days. Add broth and follow cooking instructions, allowing for an extra 20 minutes of cooking time.

To freeze cooked rolls: Drain sauce and transfer rolls to baking sheet. Freeze. When solid, wrap meal-size portions in parchment and seal each packet in heavy-duty foil. Use within 2 months. When ready to use, remove foil and parchment paper and simmer or microwave in fresh tomato sauce until heated through. Serve hot or warm.

Makes 20 servings as an appetizer, 6 to 8 as a main course.

My mother made this occasionally when we were little, mostly because she could utilize the free labor of her small children. But as my brothers got bigger, their appetites also grew while their habits became sloppier. Our mother didn't see the justice in her and their baby sister rolling all of these grape leaves just to have the boys wolf them down. So no more grape leaves.

When I went to college, I had to write an article on a rally in memoriam of the Armenian genocide. I remembered that my mother got this recipe when she was a farm girl, from the Armenian family on the next farm. The story was that my mother's Japanese-American family didn't have many friends in the community. However, the Armenian-American family also felt a bit ostracized, so they had empathy and the two families socialized and they taught my grandparents "how to be American." When Executive Order 9066 went into effect, this family bought my grandparents' farm for $1. Throughout WWII, they farmed the fields and set aside a proportional amount of the profits. When the U.S. Army finally let my mother's family return home, these amazing people sold back the farm to them for $1 and included the profits accrued during the war! They refused any praise, saying that they were just doing what was right.

Jenna Yamamoto, Bakersfield, California

SIDES & SALADS

BAKED BEANS WITH PANCETTA

There is nothing like good baked beans, and these are better than good. Every church supper cook has a favorite meat ingredient. Bacon is common. Salt pork is, too, but that has always seemed too fatty to me. Pancetta, or "Italian bacon," brings a mild smokiness to the dish that the other choices do not. Classic baked bean "garnishes" include ketchup, mustard, and pickle relish, but the only thing that anyone needs to put into these beans is a spoon. –C.S.

2 cups dried beans, picked over

¼ pound pancetta or lean salt pork, cut into 4 pieces

2 cloves garlic

2 bay leaves

¼ cup molasses

½ teaspoon ground mustard

¼ teaspoon ground ginger

salt and freshly ground black pepper, to taste

2½ cups boiling water

Cover beans with warm water. Soak overnight.

Preheat oven to 325°F.

Drain beans and discard water. Put one-third of soaked beans into an ovenproof pot with a lid. Add 1 piece of pancetta, 1 clove garlic, and 1 bay leaf. Repeat. Top with remaining beans and 2 pieces of pancetta. Pour molasses over beans.

In a bowl, combine mustard, ginger, salt and pepper, and boiling water. Stir, then pour over beans. Add additional boiling water, if necessary to just cover beans. Cover pot. Bake for 4½ to 5 hours, uncovering pot for last hour. Check liquid occasionally and top up when necessary with boiling water. Do not stir. When done, beans should be tender but hold their shape. Before serving, remove bay leaves and garlic. Serve immediately.

Makes 6 to 8 servings.

This recipe is based on one that my 94-year-old aunt sent to her 90-year-old brother when he lost his mother's bean "rule." Since my Yankee palate has been hopelessly contaminated by a number of years in Italy, I've added some unorthodox garlic and increased the number of bay leaves. My aunt's instructions ended: "You said you lost your recipe, so I put it on a card. This time, tack it up inside the cupboard door." And that's where I keep it. Almost any bean works well—Jacob's cattle, yellow-eye, soldier, navy, kidney, even Italian cannellini.

Anonymous

SIDES & SALADS

❦ OLD-FASHIONED GREEN BEANS ❧

These are well-cooked green beans, with a deep, smoky flavor; the beef broth seems to enhance this. My friend Tom, who has traveled a lot in the South, thought that it had real Southern flavor. –C.S.

4 strips bacon
1 pound fresh green beans, trimmed
1½ cups beef broth, heated
¼ cup chopped onion
freshly ground black pepper, to taste

In a skillet over medium heat, fry bacon until crisp. Remove and drain on paper towels. Reserve bacon drippings. When cool enough to handle, crumble or break up bacon.

Sauté beans in bacon drippings until bright green. Drain off fat. Add hot beef broth and onions. Heat to boiling, then reduce to simmer, cover, and cook for about 1 hour. Add pepper and bacon crumbles.

Makes 4 servings.

My grandmother grew up in Kentucky on a farm. Whenever we visited, Dad would always ask for these beans. This recipe makes me feel like I am "home."

Anonymous

Green beans are a good source of omega-3 fatty acids.

❦ BLUE CHEESE BRUSSELS SPROUTS ❧

Blue cheese goes really well with brussels sprouts. This dish is delicious and my new favorite way to have sprouts. About the almonds: Sugared almonds, to my taste, are optional. To quickly chop almonds, pulse them once or twice in a food processor. –D.T.

1 tablespoon butter
¼ cup slivered almonds
2 tablespoons sugar
5 cups brussels sprouts, trimmed
2 tablespoons olive oil, or to taste
4 ounces crumbled Danish blue cheese, divided
3 slices bacon, diced (optional)

Preheat oven to 350°F.

Melt butter in a pan over medium heat, add almonds, and sauté, stirring constantly until light brown. Pour onto a piece of aluminum foil, sprinkle with sugar, wrap up to enclose, and set aside to cool.

Arrange brussels sprouts evenly in a 13x9-inch baking dish. Drizzle with olive oil. Sprinkle with three-quarters of blue cheese. Sprinkle with sugared almonds and bacon (if using). Bake for 45 minutes, or until sprouts are tender. Top with remaining blue cheese and serve.

Makes 4 servings.

I love brussels sprouts, and my husband does not. We cook with a lot of olive oil, and my husband loves blue cheese and toasted almonds. So, I put them all together one night, and it has been a big hit. Now, I usually cook a large amount, because everyone loves them. We also sauté them in bacon drippings and add the blue cheese at the end.

Leslie Stevens, Ball Ground, Georgia

❦ BRUSSELS SPROUTS–CELERY CASSEROLE ❧

TESTER'S COMMENTS

Toasting the almonds is an option—it only takes a few seconds in the oven. Even without doing this, the results took the tasters by surprise. Those who didn't love brussels sprouts swooned over these, and people who didn't like celery were bowled over by it this way. This dish came together quickly and easily (using a jar of Alfredo sauce helped). –D.T.

1 tablespoon butter

½ cup bread crumbs

5 cups brussels sprouts, trimmed

1 bunch celery, cut into 1-inch pieces

a few drops lemon juice

2 cups Alfredo sauce (see below)

1 cup sour cream

½ cup sliced almonds

1 tablespoon chopped fresh parsley, or to taste

Preheat oven to 350°F. Grease an ovenproof casserole.

Melt butter in a pan over medium heat, add bread crumbs, and cook until toasted, stirring constantly. Set aside.

In a pot of salted water, boil brussels sprouts, celery, and lemon juice for 15 minutes, or until sprouts are almost tender. Drain and transfer to prepared casserole.

In a bowl, combine Alfredo sauce and sour cream. Pour over vegetables.

In another bowl, combine bread crumbs, almonds, and parsley and sprinkle on top. Bake for about 10 minutes, or until bubbly.

Makes 4 servings.

Almanac favorite

ALFREDO SAUCE

¼ cup (½ stick) butter

1 cup heavy cream

1 clove garlic, minced

1½ cups grated Parmesan or Gruyère cheese

¼ teaspoon ground nutmeg (optional)

¼ cup chopped fresh parsley

Melt butter. Add cream and simmer for 5 minutes. Add garlic, cheese, and nutmeg (if using) and whisk slowly, heating through. Stir in parsley. Makes 2½ cups.

❦ EGGPLANT HOAGIES ❧

Having the fixings in separate bowls made an impressive spread, and everyone loved making their own sandwich. Two diners who don't really like eggplant thought that it was really good. Others said that it "tastes like summer"—that's saying something in early March in New England. The cucumber salad was good enough to eat on its own. –D.T.

1 pound eggplant, peeled and sliced into ½-inch rounds

kosher salt

1½ cups peeled, seeded, and finely diced cucumbers

1½ cups seeded, chopped plum tomatoes

¼ cup chopped fresh parsley

½ small red onion, chopped

salt and freshly ground black pepper, to taste

peanut oil for frying

4 small hoagie or French rolls

1 cup hummus

4 hard-boiled eggs, sliced

½ cup Tahini Sauce (see below)

Sprinkle eggplant with kosher salt on both sides, place on a baking sheet or wire rack, and set aside for 30 minutes. Brush off salt and press eggplant slices firmly between paper towels to remove excess moisture.

In a bowl, combine cucumbers, tomatoes, parsley, onions, and salt and pepper. Set aside.

Heat 1 inch oil to 375°F, or very hot but not smoking. Working in batches, fry eggplant slices for 5 to 6 minutes on one side and 2 to 3 minutes on the other, or until brown and tender. Using a slotted spoon, transfer eggplant to paper towels to drain and cool.

Split hoagie rolls almost in half lengthwise. Spread 2 tablespoons hummus on each side. Divide sliced eggs, eggplant, and cucumber mixture equally among the 4 rolls. Drizzle each with 2 tablespoons Tahini Sauce.

Makes 4 sandwiches.

I love eggplant. My mother used to roast it over an open flame and make a delicious, smoky, eggplant relish with it. I make that too, but I also make these hearty fill-'em-up-fast sandwiches.

Lily Julow, Lawrenceville, Georgia

TAHINI SAUCE

Whisk together ¼ cup tahini paste with 3 tablespoons water and 1 tablespoon fresh lemon juice.
Add more water and lemon to achieve desired consistency.

SIDES & SALADS

❧ CARROT BAKE ❧

Full of veggies and quite tasty, this dish also looks pretty on the table. Plus, it comes together easily. It does it all! –D.T.

9 or 10 large carrots, peeled and cut into coins
5 tablespoons butter, divided
¼ cup chopped green bell pepper
¼ cup chopped onion
1 cup milk
2 tablespoons all-purpose flour
2 tablespoons sugar
½ teaspoon salt
½ cup soft bread crumbs

Preheat oven to 350°F. Grease an 8x8-inch baking dish.

Steam carrots until tender. Mash by hand or process in a food processor.

Melt 4 tablespoons butter in a saucepan over medium heat and cook bell peppers and onions until soft. Stir in milk, flour, sugar, and salt. Cook until thickened. Add mashed carrots. Transfer mixture to prepared baking dish.

Melt remaining 1 tablespoon butter in a skillet over medium heat. Add bread crumbs and cook, stirring, until golden. Sprinkle over carrots. Bake for 30 minutes.

Makes 6 servings.

Almanac favorite

Purée leftover cooked carrots and use to thicken soups.

GREENS AND CREAM

Here's a new way to serve greens to people who might not otherwise like them. The flavor of the coconut oil and richness of the cream combine to make the liquid taste like it is really good coconut milk. In this almost infinitely flexible recipe, Parmesan and rice are cook's option; we found kale to be delicious in this recipe all by itself. –D.T.

2 tablespoons solid coconut oil, or to taste

½ large onion, diced or sliced into rings

greens to fill a frying pan: kale, spinach, collards, turnip, mustard—or a mix

¾ cup light or heavy cream

salt, to taste

grated Parmesan cheese (optional)

In a skillet over medium heat, melt coconut oil. Add onions and cook until soft. Add greens to fill pan and cook for 5 minutes, or until greens start to wilt, stirring occasionally. Add cream and salt and reduce heat to simmer. Cook until greens wilt. Add a few tablespoons of water, if mixture becomes dry. Serve with grated Parmesan, if desired.

Makes 4 servings.

During the winter, we cook greens—particularly collards—a lot. I served greens until my husband finally said "no more." But I had fresh greens in the refrigerator, so I tried this recipe on rice, which he loves. He declared it a winner. You can also add mushrooms, clams, and/or garlic, if desired.

Brenda Blakely, Eupora, Mississippi

To help keep leafy greens fresh, put a layer of newspaper
and then a layer of paper toweling in refrigerator
bins to soak up moisture that can rot the food prematurely.

❧ PITTSBURGH POTATOES ❧

TESTER'S COMMENTS

A simple recipe with lots of flavor! Potatoes made this way complement many meat dishes well. –M.S.

5 pounds red potatoes

½ pound bacon, cooked crisp and crumbled

1 green bell pepper, chopped

1 red bell pepper, chopped

1 sweet onion, chopped

2 cups shredded cheddar cheese, divided

¾ cup mayonnaise

Preheat oven to 350°F. Grease a 13x9-inch baking dish.

Put potatoes into a pot and cover with water by at least 2 inches. Heat to a boil and cook for 20 minutes, or until fork-tender. Drain, cool, and cut into cubes.

In a bowl, combine potatoes, bacon, peppers, onions, 1 cup cheddar, and mayonnaise. Spread in prepared pan. Top with remaining cheese.

Bake for 45 minutes, or until top is bubbling.

Makes 6 to 8 servings.

When my daughter was going to college in Erie, Pennsylvania, she wanted us to cook these potatoes for her friends during finals week. She dubbed them Pittsburgh Potatoes because we are from Pittsburgh and her friends are not. They were a big hit—especially with the young men who came to eat.

Ann Lynch, New Kensington, Pennsylvania

Potatoes should never be stored in the refrigerator. Instead, keep
them in a dark, cool place at about 45° to 50°F.

"CHAMP"-STYLE MASHED POTATOES

TESTER'S COMMENTS

Irish "champ" is a flavorful combination of mashed potatoes and scallions. This very tasty recipe adds bacon. What's not to love? —M.S.

2 to 3 tablespoons butter, divided

1 clove garlic, minced

1 onion, finely chopped

½ pound bacon, sliced in half crosswise

2 pounds potatoes, peeled and sliced or cubed

heavy or light cream for mashing potatoes

2 bunches scallions, washed and trimmed

salt and freshly ground black pepper, to taste

In a skillet over medium heat, melt 1 tablespoon butter. Add garlic and onions and cook until transparent. Remove garlic and onions from pan and set aside. Add bacon and cook until crispy; drain on paper towels and crumble.

Put potatoes into a pot and cover with water by at least 2 inches. Heat to a boil and cook for 25 to 30 minutes, or until fork-tender. Drain and mash with remaining butter and cream.

Transfer mashed potatoes to a serving bowl. Using kitchen scissors, snip scallions into ½-inch lengths over potatoes. Add bacon, onions, and garlic. Mix lightly and season with salt and pepper.

Makes 6 servings.

Almanac favorite

Do not overmash potatoes. Doing so releases starch
and gives the potatoes a glue-like consistency.

CHEESY POTATOES

Here's a new twist on scalloped potatoes that had even my finicky eaters coming back for more. –M.S.

½ cup (1 stick) butter, melted
12 to 14 russet potatoes, peeled and thinly sliced
salt and freshly ground black pepper, to taste
4 cups shredded sharp cheddar cheese
½ cup plain fine bread crumbs

Preheat oven to 350°F. Spray a 13x9-inch baking dish with nonstick spray.

Pour melted butter into bottom of prepared baking dish. Put potatoes into baking dish, season with salt and pepper, and toss to coat. Arrange potatoes in layers. Sprinkle with cheddar to cover. Sprinkle bread crumbs over the cheddar. Bake for 1 hour.

Serves 8 to 10.

My mother came up with this recipe, and it is one of my favorites. It's simple to make. The bread crumbs and cheese topping turn this dish into an extra special one. My family and friends love it and ask for it often.

Lisa Turpin, Stanford, Kentucky

Russet potatoes are sometimes called baking or Idaho potatoes.

SIDES & SALADS

MASHED POTATOES FROM INDIA

Wicked easy! If you are not used to coconut oil, you should add it 1 tablespoon at a time, not all four at once, and taste. Coconut oil is an acquired taste, but it makes the potatoes really creamy. –S.P.

1 pound potatoes

½ cup fresh mint leaves, pounded with mortar and pestle

pinch of ground turmeric

sea salt and freshly ground black pepper, to taste

paprika, to taste

seeds of 1 cardamom pod

4 tablespoons coconut oil

Put potatoes into a pot and cover with water by at least 2 inches. Heat to a boil and cook for 30 minutes, or until fork-tender. Drain, peel, and mash potatoes. Add mint, turmeric, salt, pepper, paprika, cardamom, and coconut oil and stir well. Let rest for 45 minutes to allow flavors to meld.

Makes 2 to 4 servings.

When I came to this country as a foreign student, my budget was meager. I created these mashed potatoes with what was in the kitchen. The key to the flavor of the potatoes is the mint, which is pounded in a mortar. Finely chopping the mint with a steel knife produces a flavor different from the one that comes from being pounded in a mortar. Tools in the kitchen enable or disable flavor. The end.

Annina John, Union City, New Jersey

Coconut oil comes in jars in solid form. If a recipe calls for melted coconut oil, place the entire jar in a bowl of very warm water. As the oil melts, pour out as much as you need.

GALE'S SWEET POTATOES

TESTER'S COMMENTS

I needed only 3 tablespoons of pineapple juice and 3 tablespoons of sweet potato water for drizzling. This dish is just sweet enough, and it goes well with turkey, chicken, or ham. –M.S.

4 medium sweet potatoes

1 can (20 ounces) pineapple tidbits, drained, liquid reserved

4 tablespoons (½ stick) butter, divided

3 tablespoons brown sugar

½ cup coarsely chopped pecans

Cover sweet potatoes with water and boil until fork-tender. Remove from water, reserve cooking water, and set aside. When cool enough to handle, peel, then cut into cubes.

In a bowl, mix together 3 to 4 tablespoons sweet potato water and 3 to 4 tablespoons reserved pineapple juice.

Preheat oven to 350°F. Grease a 2-quart baking dish with 1 tablespoon butter. Transfer sweet potatoes and pineapple to prepared baking dish and stir to combine.

Dice the remaining 3 tablespoons butter and distribute over sweet potatoes. Sprinkle with brown sugar. Drizzle with juice mixture. Sprinkle pecans on top. Bake for 30 minutes, or until bubbly.

Makes 6 to 8 servings.

I do not care for marshmallow-topped sweet potatoes. I also had gotten tired of substitutes of "naked" sweet potatoes just sitting in a bowl. So, I thought about what I liked and how I could make it. This was my creation. Everyone I've served it to has loved it and requested Gale's Sweet Potatoes for potlucks.

Gale Green, Silver City, New Mexico

GARLIC-MASHED SWEET POTATOES

TESTER'S COMMENTS

Who knew that these two garden greats paired so well? Roasting the garlic mellows and sweetens it, and then the jam-like consistency of the garlic cloves enlivens the sweet potatoes. –D.T.

2 large sweet potatoes, washed

1 tablespoon olive oil, plus more for oiling sweet potatoes

1 head garlic

¼ cup (½ stick) butter

salt and freshly ground black pepper, to taste

Preheat oven to 350°F. Spray a roasting pan with nonstick cooking spray.

Pierce sweet potatoes with a fork and oil the skins. Place in roasting pan.

Cut top off garlic head. Place in garlic roaster or on aluminum foil. Pour 1 tablespoon olive oil on garlic. Cover roaster or wrap up foil.

Bake sweet potatoes and garlic for about 1 hour, or until sweet potatoes are soft. Peel, then cut up sweet potatoes.

Push garlic out of skins. Add to sweet potatoes, with butter. Mash until fluffy. Season with salt and pepper.

Makes 6 servings.

Almanac favorite

Yams and sweet potatoes often cause confusion. True yams are from the plant family Dioscoreaceae. They are huge tubers with rough, scaly skin, grown mostly in West Africa and tropical Asia. Sweet potatoes, from the morning glory family, are not tubers but fleshy roots native to Central and South America. Depending on the variety, they can have dry or moist flesh in colors ranging from white to yellow, orange, red, and even purple.

❧ SCALLOPED TOMATOES ❧

TESTER'S COMMENTS

Having fresh plum and regular "winter" tomatoes at hand, I used them instead of canned tomatoes. Cooking them on the stovetop before baking would have made them more like canned-quality, but I was glad that I had not. The dish was a hit: The soft chunks of tomato were scrumptious. (In-season tomatoes would be best!) About half the sugar suggested would be adequate, or use no sugar, if you prefer a more tart tomato taste. –D.T.

1 can (14.5 ounces) diced tomatoes, with liquid, or 1 can (14.5 ounces) whole tomatoes, diced, with liquid

⅔ cup sugar

30 Saltine crackers, crushed

6 tablespoons (¾ stick) butter, melted

Preheat oven to 350°F.

In a bowl, combine tomatoes and sugar. Pour into a 10x7-inch baking dish. Spread cracker crumbs evenly over tomatoes. Pour butter over crumbs. Bake for 30 minutes.

Makes 6 to 8 servings.

This is a recipe that my grandmother and my mother passed down. To me, this is far tastier than scalloped tomatoes with bread crumb topping and a lot easier to prepare.

Cathey Finger, Lincolnton, North Carolina

In colonial times, people thought that tomatoes were toxic and called them "poison apples."

❧ ROASTED THYMED VEGGIES ❧

I roast vegetables often. This particular mix, with dried thyme, is excellent. Roasting times for different vegetables can be tricky, but not here. The two vegetables I care about most were perfect: the potatoes soft and the bell peppers not cooked to mush. –D.T.

4 to 6 small red potatoes, chopped into bite-size pieces

3 carrots, sliced into coins

olive oil

1 teaspoon dried thyme or 1 tablespoon chopped fresh thyme, divided

dried onion flakes, to taste

garlic powder, to taste

salt and freshly ground black pepper, to taste

10 mushrooms, sliced

1 head broccoli, cut into florets

1 red bell pepper, sliced

Preheat oven to 350°F.

In a bowl, combine potatoes and carrots. Sprinkle with olive oil and ½ teaspoon dried thyme, onion flakes, garlic powder, and salt and pepper. Mix well. Transfer to a baking dish. Cook for 20 minutes.

Combine mushrooms, broccoli, and bell pepper. Sprinkle with olive oil, remaining thyme, onion flakes, garlic powder, and salt and pepper. Add to potato–carrot mixture, stir, and bake for 10 to 15 minutes more.

Makes 4 servings.

I acquired an allergy to lots of foods and spices and had to create something that I could eat instead. You can make it your own according to your family's likes and whatever is fresh from your garden: Add any other veggies you desire. (Cook firmer vegetables with the potatoes and carrots and add the softer ones as directed.) You can add basil, rosemary, and/or oregano, but thyme is what makes this recipe so yummy.

Sandy Dershem, Yale, Oklahoma

When substituting dried herbs for fresh, use one-third of the fresh amount. For example, 1 tablespoon of chopped fresh herbs equals 1 teaspoon of dried herbs.

Vegan or Vegetarian Tourtière

As someone who was raised vegetarian, I've never had a "meat" pie like this, traditional or vegetarian. This is hearty and satisfying. Even if you are not vegetarian or vegan, you will be pleasantly surprised. Options: Use a store-bought piecrust, if convenient, and/or serve this dish with spicy brown mustard. –D.T.

1 tablespoon vegan butter

¼ cup chopped onion

1 tube (14 ounces) lean vegetarian ground sausage

1 package (12 ounces) vegetarian meatless crumbles

1 large potato, peeled and diced

1 teaspoon salt, or to taste

1 teaspoon freshly ground black pepper

¼ teaspoon ground nutmeg

¼ teaspoon ground allspice

1 cup bread crumbs

2 discs pâte brisée or vegan piecrust dough

Preheat oven to 350°F. Grease a pie plate.

In a saucepan over medium heat, melt butter and cook onions until fragrant. Add vegetarian ground sausage, meatless crumbles, and potatoes. Add salt, pepper, nutmeg, allspice, and 1½ cups water. Mix well. Cook for 15 to 20 minutes, stirring often and adding more water, ¼ cup at a time, if necessary to keep ingredients from sticking to pan. Remove from heat and add bread crumbs. Mix well.

Roll out both dough discs. Line bottom of pie plate with one disc. Spread filling in it. Cover with remaining disc. Cut three small vents on top for steam to escape. Bake for 35 to 40 minutes, or until crust is golden brown. Serve warm.

Makes 10 to 12 servings.

My aunts worked really hard to re-create the meat version of this dish. My great-memere never wrote down the recipe; it was created by memory and taste. Every Christmas, we get together to make these pies for friends and family. It is tradition for the younger ones to learn about our family history and tourtière-making. They join us and sit at the table for piecrust duty. When I became vegan, I was a bit sad to miss out on our family tradition. The family tourtière is one of the first recipes that I "veganized."

Heather Poire, Laconia, New Hampshire

A traditional tourtière is a meat pie, but this version is nonmeat; it uses textured vegetable protein (TVP), which usually contains a soy product.

❧ GOLDEN ROMESCO ❧

What beautiful color in this delicious dish! I served it over pan-fried tofu with vegetables and, later, on pasta. Be sure to grind the almonds; this adds to the texture. In summer, with fresh, ripe tomatoes, I will make it again and again. —D.T.

2 ripe yellow or golden tomatoes

2 yellow bell peppers

¼ cup extra-virgin olive oil, divided

2 cloves garlic

¾ cup sliced blanched almonds, toasted

kosher salt and freshly ground black pepper, to taste

Preheat oven to 425°F. Line a baking sheet with aluminum foil.

Slice tomatoes in half and place cut sides up on foil. Set whole bell peppers on foil. Roast for 40 minutes, rotating peppers at least twice, or until brown spots appear on peppers' skin and tomatoes are soft. Set aside. When cool enough to handle, remove and discard the skins and seeds from tomatoes and peppers; remove stems from peppers.

In a skillet over medium heat, warm 1 tablespoon of olive oil. Mash garlic and add to skillet. Cook until lightly toasted.

Put toasted almonds into a food processor and process until powdery. Add tomatoes, peppers, garlic, and remaining oil and process until smooth. Season with salt and pepper.

Makes 2 to 3 cups or 4 to 6 servings.

We use Romesco on our seared sea scallops and sautéed tripletail combination. It adds a bright and different Catalonian twist to South Florida seafood.

Neil Griffin, Florida

SIDES & SALADS

GHIVETCH

If you do not wish to cook the rice in the veggie layers, you can cook it separately and serve it on the side. Either way, this delicious dish resembles a vegetable pot pie, minus the crust. –D.T.

4 yellow onions, sliced

4 waxy potatoes, such as Yukon Gold, peeled and cut into chunks

1 sweet potato, peeled and cut into chunks

2 stalks celery, sliced

1 package (12 ounces) frozen green peas, thawed, or equal fresh

1 package (12 ounces) frozen cut green beans, thawed, or equal fresh

⅓ cup vegetable oil

kosher salt and freshly ground black pepper, to taste

pinch of sugar

4 carrots, peeled and cut into chunks

1 green bell pepper, seeded and sliced

1 cup uncooked long-grain rice

1 eggplant, peeled and cut into chunks

6 to 8 ripe tomatoes, stemmed and cut into chunks

Preheat oven to 350°F.

Layer ingredients in roasting pan in the order listed. Cover tightly with aluminum foil and cook for 2 hours. Uncover and mix lightly. Texture should be medium-chunky and firmest vegetables fork-tender. Return to oven and cook, uncovered, 30 minutes more, or until top layer is golden brown.

Makes 8 to10 servings.

This classic Romanian harvest dish has been in my family for three generations and came from an aunt who married into a Romanian family. It's delicious and "meaty"-tasting, although it contains no meat. The recipe makes a whole lot and freezes very well. It may need more salt when thawed and reheated. Layer the ingredients exactly as listed.

Lily Julow, Lawrenceville, Georgia

SIDES & SALADS

APPLE SLAW WITH HONEY MUSTARD VINAIGRETTE

TESTER'S COMMENTS

This slaw certainly pleased my tasters (and me)! The sweetness of the apple and honey complements the green onions, mustard, and vinegar. The dressing is light, but flavorful—simply delicious. –D.T.

Dressing:

3 tablespoons honey

2 tablespoons apple cider vinegar

1 teaspoon spicy brown mustard

½ teaspoon salt

2 tablespoons canola oil

Slaw:

4 cups homemade or packaged coleslaw

1 cup chopped Gala or other red apple

2 tablespoons sliced green onion

For dressing: In a bowl, whisk together honey, vinegar, mustard, salt, and canola oil.

For slaw: In another bowl, combine coleslaw, apples, and green onions.

Pour dressing over slaw and toss to coat. Chill before serving.

Makes 10 servings.

I make this in the summer for potlucks, and it's always a people pleaser.

Sharon Whisler, Fremont, Nebraska

To make your own coleslaw mix, shred ½ head of cabbage and 2 carrots.

✿ MOM'S COLESLAW ✿

TESTER'S COMMENTS

While this slaw tastes like traditional coleslaw, it's a bit "lighter" because the dressing uses so little mayonnaise—and that was a welcome change. –D.T.

Slaw:

2 carrots, shredded

½ head cabbage, finely shredded

½ stalk celery, minced

¼ onion, minced

Dressing:

2 tablespoons mayonnaise

1 teaspoon white vinegar

1 teaspoon red-wine vinegar

½ teaspoon brown mustard

⅛ teaspoon paprika

1 packet Splenda

pinch of salt and freshly ground black pepper

¼ cup half-and-half

For slaw: In a bowl, combine carrots, cabbage, celery, and onions and set aside.

For dressing: In another bowl, combine mayonnaise, vinegars, mustard, paprika, Splenda, and salt and pepper. Whisk to blend. Drizzle in half-and-half slowly, whisking until thick.

Pour over slaw mixture and stir to coat. Cover and refrigerate for at least 1 hour before serving.

Makes 4 to 6 servings.

My mom has always made this slaw to put over her hotdogs or BBQ sandwiches. I only altered it with the Splenda because my husband is diabetic. I think it comes out so much better with this substitution because you get no undissolved grit from the sugar.

Kelly Light, St. Petersburg, Florida

The word "coleslaw" comes from the Dutch word *koolsla,* meaning cabbage salad.

THREE BEAN SALAD WITH ARTICHOKE HEARTS, OLIVES, AND FETA

Dressing:

¼ cup olive oil

2 tablespoons white-wine vinegar

2 tablespoons balsamic vinegar

1 teaspoon sugar

½ teaspoon salt

Salad:

1 can (14 ounces) pinto beans, drained and rinsed

1 can (14 ounces) kidney beans, drained and rinsed

1 can (14 ounces) garbanzo beans, drained and rinsed

1 can (14 ounces) artichoke hearts, chopped

4 scallions, thinly sliced (white and light green parts only)

1 red bell pepper, diced

½ red onion, diced

½ cup chopped kalamata olives

¾ cup crumbled feta cheese

salt and freshly ground black pepper, to taste

For dressing: In a bowl, whisk together olive oil and vinegars. Add sugar and salt and whisk until smooth.

For salad: In another bowl, combine beans, artichoke hearts, scallions, bell peppers, onions, olives, and feta. Toss to combine, then season with salt and pepper.

Pour dressing over salad and toss to combine. Cover and refrigerate for several hours or overnight. Serve cold.

Makes 8 servings.

As a vegetarian, I've eaten countless versions of three bean salads, but I've never liked that green beans were included—so I made up my own recipe. I eat this as a side dish and especially like to use it as the base for a tasty wrap sandwich with spinach, baby romaine, and sometimes a little hummus. Both ways are great when it's too hot to cook.

Aimee Seavey, Manchester, New Hampshire

HOT BEAN SALAD

Make sure not to overcook the beans. They still need to crunch when you bite into them. —M.A.J.

3 strips bacon

¾ cup diced onion

1 pound fresh yellow string beans, preferably, or green, or a mixture, French-cut or sliced thinly across

1½ tablespoons apple cider vinegar, or to taste

1½ cups sour cream

ground white pepper, to taste

3 tablespoons chopped fresh dill (optional)

In a skillet over medium heat, fry bacon until crisp. Remove and drain on paper towels. Reserve bacon drippings. When cool enough to handle, crumble or break up bacon.

Sauté onions in bacon drippings until just soft. Add beans and cook briefly until al dente. Add vinegar and stir briefly. Remove from heat and stir in sour cream. (Do not let sour cream curdle.) Taste, and add more vinegar, if desired. Season with white pepper and chopped dill (if using). Garnish with crumbled bacon. Serve warm or at room temperature.

Makes 4 servings.

This salad comes from the cooking style of a people who had little meat and is probably inspired by German Hot Potato Salad. It came from the mind of my nearly illiterate maternal grandmother, Elizabeth Mohr—"Nana" to me. Nana was born Elizabeth Pfeifer in the village of Zbora, Austria, near the Hungarian border, on January 31, 1886, and escaped with her parents to Winnipeg, Manitoba, on May 24, 1891. After her husband, George Mohr, died, Nana came to Medicine Hat, Alberta, in 1941 to live with and take care of my ailing aunt and her family. Nana died in her sleep while watching television at her retirement home. Her recipes did not die with her, because she had taught her grandchildren to cook. This is a favorite of ours and of every kid who has ever tried it.

Bob Scammell, Red Deer, Alberta

White vinegar can be substituted for apple cider vinegar in recipes.

BLUEBERRY–KIDNEY BEAN SALAD WITH FRESH VEGETABLES

You'll find many ways to enjoy this, including as a side dish with pork, beef, or chicken. It can also be served on top of cooked pasta. –M.A.J.

Dressing:

¼ cup olive oil

½ cup apple cider vinegar

1 teaspoon salt

½ teaspoon freshly ground black pepper

¼ teaspoon curry powder

Salad:

1 can (15.5 ounces) red kidney beans, drained and rinsed

1 onion, cut into bite-size pieces

1 tomato, cut into bite-size pieces

1 green bell pepper, cut into bite-size pieces

1½ cups fresh blueberries

¼ cup crumbled feta cheese

For dressing: In a bowl, whisk together olive oil, vinegar, salt, pepper, and curry powder.

For salad: In another bowl, combine beans, onions, tomatoes, and peppers. Stir in blueberries and feta.

Pour dressing over bean mixture and mix well. Cover and refrigerate for at least 1 hour before serving.

Makes 4 servings.

First-prize winner in the 2014 *Old Farmer's Almanac Garden Guide* Reader Recipe Contest for berries
Oscar Righetti, Bracebridge, Ontario

Do not rinse blueberries until you are ready to use them.

❧ SWEET 'N' SUNNY CAULIFLOWER SALAD ❧

TESTER'S COMMENTS

The sunflower mayo was a delicious surprise and I used what was leftover on a spinach salad later in the week. –M.A.J.

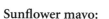

Sunflower mayo:

½ teaspoon ground mustard

¼ teaspoon salt

¼ teaspoon ground paprika

⅛ teaspoon cayenne pepper

¼ cup refrigerated egg substitute

2 tablespoons white vinegar or fresh lemon juice

2 cups sunflower oil, divided

Cauliflower salad:

1 cup sunflower mayo or store-bought mayo

½ cup Parmesan cheese

¼ cup sugar

1½ teaspoons freshly ground black pepper

1 large cauliflower, trimmed and cut into small florets (about 8 cups)

1 medium red onion, thinly sliced

1½ cups shredded mozzarella cheese

6 slices bacon, fried until crisp and then crumbled

¼ cup sunflower kernels

For sunflower mayo: In a bowl, combine mustard, salt, paprika, and cayenne. Add egg substitute and vinegar. Beat with electric mixer until blended. With mixer running, add 6 teaspoons oil, one at a time, then slowly pour remaining oil in a thin, steady stream. Cover and refrigerate for up to 2 weeks.

Makes about 2 cups.

For cauliflower salad: In another bowl, combine sunflower mayo with Parmesan, sugar, and pepper. Add cauliflower and onions and toss to coat. Add mozzarella and stir. Refrigerate until cold.

Mix in bacon and sunflower kernels just before serving.

Makes 6 to 8 servings.

This cool and savory salad makes a great addition to a lunch buffet or potluck dinner. Use purple, orange, or green cauliflower for a colorful twist. The mayo recipe makes more than you will need for this salad; use the extra as a sandwich spread or dressing for a leafy green salad.

Tamra Kriedeman, Enderlin, North Dakota

❧ Grama's Mixed Vegetable Salad ❧

TESTER'S COMMENTS

I brought this salad to a party in the winter, and everyone who tasted it loved it. It gets an A+! –L.R.

1 teaspoon salt

¾ cup red-wine vinegar

½ cup vegetable oil

1 cup sugar

1 teaspoon freshly ground black pepper

1 can (14.5 ounces) French-cut green beans, drained

1 can (11 ounces) white corn, drained

1 can (5 ounces) baby peas (Le Sueur brand with the silver label), drained

1 green bell pepper, chopped

1 cup chopped onion

1 cup chopped celery

In a saucepan over medium-high heat, combine salt, vinegar, oil, sugar, pepper, and 1 teaspoon water. Heat to a boil.

In a bowl, combine green beans, corn, and peas. Add chopped bell peppers, onions, and celery. Add boiled dressing and stir to coat. Cover and let stand for 8 hours or overnight. Do not refrigerate for this period.

Makes about 6 servings.

My grandmother used to make this all the time. She would use a strainer-type spoon to get all the vegetables out. When there was just "juice" left, she would heat that up, pour it over spinach (to make a "wilted" salad), and then top the salad with riced hard-boiled egg. It's one of the many recipes that made happy childhood memories for me. This recipe can be doubled.

Lori Spielman, Glendale, Wisconsin

When buying bell peppers, choose firm, richly colored
ones that are the heaviest for their size.

TRADITIONAL POTATO SALAD

TESTER'S COMMENTS

Yellow mustard and relish are a must for potato salad, in my book. I especially like that this recipe uses both mayonnaise and Miracle Whip. It is a really good traditional potato salad, and the recipe can easily be halved. –C.S.

3 pounds potatoes

6 hard-boiled eggs

2 stalks celery, with leaves, finely diced

1 small onion, finely diced

¼ cup dill pickle relish or finely diced dill pickles

¼ cup finely diced green or yellow bell pepper (optional)

1 teaspoon salt, plus more, to taste

½ teaspoon freshly ground black pepper, plus more, to taste

½ teaspoon celery seeds

1 cup mayonnaise

½ cup Miracle Whip

¼ cup milk

2 tablespoons yellow mustard

paprika, for sprinkling

Put potatoes into a pot, cover with water by at least 2 inches, and salt the water. Heat to a boil and cook for 30 minutes, or until a paring knife can easily pierce potatoes to center (skins may also start to crack). Drain and set aside to cool slightly.

Peel potatoes and remove any eyes or bad spots. Do not rinse. Cut into bite-size chunks and place in a bowl.

Peel eggs, reserve three yolks, dice remainder, and sprinkle on top of potatoes. Add celery, onions, relish, bell peppers (if using), 1 teaspoon salt, ½ teaspoon pepper, and celery seeds.

In another bowl, mash reserved egg yolks with a fork. Add mayonnaise, Miracle Whip, milk, and mustard. Mix until smooth. Taste and adjust salt and pepper, if necessary. Pour over potatoes, then gently fold until ingredients are coated, being careful not to mash potatoes. Sprinkle with paprika. Chill before serving.

Makes 12 servings.

I took features that I liked from my mother's potato salad recipe and combined them with some that I liked from the recipes of two friends to make this one great recipe for myself.

Rhonda Sine

ℰ POTATO SALAD WITH GREEN BEANS AND CHICKEN ℒ

TESTER'S COMMENTS

With or without chicken, add some crusty bread, and you've got a complete meal. –J.S.

½ cup olive oil

¼ cup white-wine vinegar

1 clove garlic, minced

salt and freshly ground black pepper, to taste

2 pounds potatoes, peeled, cooked, and still
    warm

½ cup chopped fresh parsley

½ cup chopped red onion

6 boneless, skinless chicken breast halves, grilled
    just until tender, sliced

1 pound green beans, cooked until crisp-tender

cherry tomato halves, for garnish

In a bowl, combine olive oil, vinegar, garlic, and salt and pepper and blend until smooth.

Slice warm potatoes and place in another bowl. Pour oil–vinegar dressing over potatoes and toss gently. Sprinkle with parsley and red onions and toss again. Taste and add more salt and pepper, if desired. Add chicken and cooked beans to potatoes and mix gently. Garnish with cherry tomatoes.

Makes 6 servings.

Almanac favorite

To eliminate garlic smell on your hands, rub them
on something made of stainless steel, such as a pan, spoon, or sink.

SIDES & SALADS

❧ HONEY FRENCH ❧ DRESSING

TESTER'S COMMENTS

This is lovely on greens, and—with 1 tablespoon of lemon pepper added—delightful on spinach–strawberry salad. I recommend warming the mixture in the jar in the microwave for 10 to 15 seconds before shaking to combine the ingredients. This helps the mixture to blend and brings out the vinegar flavor. –C.S.

⅓ cup honey (local is best)
⅓ cup red-wine or apple cider vinegar
⅓ cup vegetable oil
¼ teaspoon salt

In a jar with a lid, combine honey, vinegar, oil, and salt. Shake to blend. Splash over your favorite greens.

Makes 1 cup.

The original recipe came from a small booklet of honey recipes that I sent for over 40 years ago. I always make it from the honey that my beekeeper husband provides.

Marie DeRoy, Smithfield, Rhode Island

❧ MY FAVORITE SALAD ❧ DRESSING

TESTER'S COMMENTS

Everyone needs a good, reliable dressing. Sweeten to taste, not all at once. Add the sugar slowly, tasting as you go. Like me, you may prefer less than 1 cup. –C.S.

1 cup olive oil
1 tablespoon tarragon vinegar (optional)
1 tablespoon Worcestershire sauce
1 teaspoon salt
1 shallot, diced
paprika, to taste
½ cup white-wine vinegar
1 cup sugar, or to taste

In a jar with a lid, combine olive oil, tarragon vinegar (if using), Worcestershire sauce, salt, shallot, and paprika. Shake to blend.

In a saucepan, heat white-wine vinegar and sugar to a boil and cook until sugar dissolves. Add to the jar and shake to combine.

Makes 2 cups.

I first had this salad dressing when my best friend from Maryland and her family taught me how to eat Maryland crabs. Her mom, Rhona, made a similar dressing for a salad of baby spinach, dried cranberries, feta cheese, and sliced almonds. This goes great with a loaf of crusty bread, lots of Maryland crabs, and good company!

Lindsay Forcino, Malvern, Pennsylvania

❧ ZUCCHINI PEPPER RELISH ❧

TESTER'S COMMENTS

This colorful condiment goes great with crackers and cheese or even vegetable stew. Fair warning: It is a bit sweet. –D.T.

1 medium to large zucchini

6 bell peppers, orange, yellow, red, or a combination, diced

4 sweet onions, diced

3½ cups sugar

1½ cups white vinegar

2 tablespoons cornstarch

1 teaspoon ground turmeric

1 teaspoon ground mustard

Grate or shred zucchini to make 3 cups.

In a stainless steel pot, combine zucchini, bell peppers, onions, sugar, vinegar, cornstarch, turmeric, and mustard. Heat to a boil, stirring, then maintain a simmer. Stir occasionally, until onions are clear and relish is thick. Remove from heat. Pour into sterilized jars, seal, and process in a boiling-water bath for 10 minutes.

Makes 6 to 7 pints.

I had way too many zucchini in my garden and lots of peppers and wanted to incorporate both for a fabulous flavor. These vegetables are gorgeous in a jar as a gift and can be used on any meat for added flavor.

Susan Lawrence, Ontario

Orange, yellow, and red bell peppers are actually just green
bell peppers that were left on the plant to mature.

VEGETABLE RELISH, OR MAWMAW'S TRASH RELISH

TESTER'S COMMENTS

Here's an ideal use for "extra" end-of-season vegetables. It has great taste and really satisfies as a snack at the end of a hot day in the garden. Be sure to put a jar away for mid-January, when you're perusing seed catalogs and dreaming about next year's plot. –D.T.

7 cups diced zucchini

3 cups diced yellow squash

1 cup seeded and diced cucumber

1 cup shredded carrots

3 or 4 banana peppers, diced

1 red bell pepper, diced

1 green bell pepper, diced

6 cups sugar

1 quart white vinegar

1 teaspoon ground turmeric

1 teaspoon ground mustard

1 teaspoon celery seed

1 teaspoon canning salt

½ teaspoon red pepper flakes

Put zucchini, yellow squash, cucumbers, carrots, and peppers into a bowl of cold water.

In a pot over medium heat, combine sugar, vinegar, turmeric, mustard, celery seed, salt, red pepper flakes, and 2 cups water. Heat until sugar dissolves.

Drain vegetables. Add to vinegar mixture. Heat to a boil and simmer for 15 minutes, or until tender. Transfer vegetables to sterilized jars. Add vinegar mixture to cover. Seal and process in a boiling-water bath for 10 minutes.

Makes about 15 pints.

Everyone knows how abundantly zucchini squashes grow in the garden. I was raised on a farm, where everything was eaten or canned for later in the year. I had zucchini that we just could not eat, so I decided to can them. This is a hit with everyone who eats it. Serve it with fish, chicken, hot dogs, hamburgers, vegetables. I even put it out one night at a potluck, and they ate it with corn chips as a dip. I add whatever vegetables I have at that particular time of year, and it is always eaten. I sometimes have vinegar mixture left over and put it in a jar in the refrigerator. I add vegetables to this and use it as a relish. My family calls it Mawmaw's trash relish.

Linda Harrison, Cairo, Georgia

SIDES & SALADS

❧ SOFRITO ❧

A foundation in Spanish and Caribbean cooking, sofrito (soe-FREE-toe) explodes with flavor. Use as salsa, with chips, or as a "bright" addition to soups, beans, or rice. Experiment with ingredients: Roma, or "plum," tomatoes are not as juicy as slicers. Try different peppers and onions, too, and if it's all that you've got, make do with the herbs that you have on hand. –J.S.

5 cloves garlic

3 tomatoes, roughly chopped

1 red onion, roughly chopped

1 red bell pepper, roughly chopped

1 green bell pepper, roughly chopped

1 bunch fresh chives, roughly chopped

1 bunch fresh oregano, stemmed and roughly chopped

1 bunch fresh cilantro, stemmed and roughly chopped

1 bunch fresh parsley, stemmed and roughly chopped

Place garlic, tomatoes, onions, peppers, chives, oregano, cilantro, and parsley in a food processor. Process in quick bursts, then for 30 to 60 seconds, or until as chunky or pulverized as you like. If you start with tomatoes, you should not need to add water; the tomatoes add enough juice.

Makes about 2 cups, depending on size of vegetables.

I make a large batch of this and then freeze it in smaller containers. I always keep a working batch thawed in my fridge.

Sheilla I. Parkerson, Jaffrey, New Hampshire

Did you know? Cilantro tastes like soap to 1 in 7 people.

SOUPS, CHOWDERS, & CHILIS

❧ HEARTY BEAN AND KALE SOUP ❧

I didn't have a ham bone, so the meat cutter suggested that I use a ham slice. I cut the ham in pieces, and it was a very good substitute. Tim's mom and the meat cutter know how to make a good soup! –L.R.

1 tablespoon olive oil

4 cloves garlic, minced

1 yellow onion, chopped

2 cups raw kale, stems removed, chopped

2 stalks celery, chopped

2 carrots, sliced

1 ham bone

6 cups chicken broth

2 cans (15 ounces each) navy beans, drained and rinsed

2 cans (15 ounces each) black beans, drained and rinsed

1 can (28 ounces) diced tomatoes, with juice

1 bay leaf

2 teaspoons dried thyme

salt and freshly ground black pepper, to taste

1 cup chopped fresh parsley

shredded Parmesan cheese, for topping

Heat olive oil in a soup pot. Add garlic and onions and sauté until soft and translucent. Add kale, celery, and carrots and sauté for 15 minutes. Add ham bone, chicken broth, beans, tomatoes, bay leaf, thyme, salt and pepper, and parsley and simmer for 1 hour. Remove bay leaf. Serve with crusty bread and pass Parmesan at the table.

Makes 6 servings.

This is Mom's recipe.

Tim Olson, Mora, Minnesota

CRANBERRY BEAN SOUP

TESTER'S COMMENTS

This hearty soup hit the spot on a cold winter day. Don't skip the Parmesan cheese—it is the perfect finishing touch. –S.L.P.

2 cups dried cranberry beans
1 cup whole dried peas
1 meaty ham bone
2 bay leaves
1 onion, peeled and stuck with 4 cloves
5 potatoes, peeled and chopped
4 leeks, white part only, chopped, or 3 onions, chopped
3 cloves garlic, minced
2 carrots, peeled and chopped
grated Parmesan cheese, to taste

Soak beans and peas overnight in water to cover. Drain.

Place beans and peas in a soup pot with 3 quarts water, ham bone, bay leaves, and whole onion. Bring to a boil, reduce heat, cover, and simmer for 2 hours, or until beans and peas are tender.

Remove ham bone, chop meat into small bits, discard bone, and return meat to pot. Add potatoes, leeks, garlic, and carrots. Simmer, partially covered, for 30 minutes, or until vegetables are tender. Remove bay leaves and clove-stuck onion. Garnish each portion with grated Parmesan.

Makes 6 to 8 servings.

Almanac favorite

SPECIAL BLUE CHEESE SOUP

TESTER'S COMMENTS

Because I used my food processor, my soup had teeny bits of cabbage and cauliflower in it. It was not creamy, but I enjoyed the texture. Some tasters thought that the blue cheese gave it enough flavor, but "bleu" fans might prefer a few pieces sprinkled on their serving. Overall, it's easy and delicious and freezes well. –J.S.

½ head cabbage
½ head cauliflower
1 quart chicken broth
2 ounces crumbled blue cheese
salt and freshly ground black pepper, to taste

Roughly chop cabbage. Separate cauliflower florets from stems. Steam cabbage and cauliflower for about 10 minutes, or until tender. Combine cabbage, cauliflower, chicken broth, and blue cheese in a high-speed blender and run on high for 5 to 6 minutes. Season with salt and pepper.

Makes 4 servings.

This is a delicious soup that I made up after buying a high-performance blender. Everyone I have served this soup to has asked for the recipe. It's really easy and a great cold weather meal.

John Weaver, Alliance, Ohio

CARROT GINGER SOUP

TESTER'S COMMENTS

The sweetness of carrots and spiciness of ginger work well together in this soup. Try to blend out as many lumps as you can—the velvety texture adds another level to the taste. –S.L.P.

2 tablespoons (¼ stick) butter or margarine

2 leeks, chopped

1 pound carrots, peeled and diced

1 pound potatoes, peeled and diced

1 orange, zest and juice

1 teaspoon chopped fresh ginger

1 teaspoon brown sugar

4 cups vegetable broth

1 cup milk

salt, to taste

dash of dry sherry, to taste

dash of ground nutmeg, to taste

chopped fresh parsley or cilantro, for garnish

Melt butter in a soup pot over medium heat. Add leeks and cook until soft and translucent. Add carrots, potatoes, orange zest and juice, ginger, and brown sugar. Cook for 5 to 7 minutes, or until softened.

Add broth and milk and simmer for 20 minutes.

Transfer to a blender or food processor and purée in batches. Return to soup pot. Season with salt, sherry, and nutmeg. Serve garnished with chopped fresh parsley.

Makes 4 to 6 servings.

First-prize winner in *The 2014 Old Farmer's Almanac* Reader Recipe Contest for carrots
Ann Fine, Kansas City, Missouri

In a pinch, ground ginger can be substituted for fresh ginger.
For 1 teaspoon chopped fresh ginger, substitute ¼ teaspoon ground ginger.

SOUPS, CHOWDERS, & CHILIS

❧ ROASTED VEGETABLE SOUP ❧

TESTER'S COMMENTS

If you love vegetables, you'll love this. The "soupiness" depends entirely on your preference: Lots of veggies may require more liquid. For really thick soup, less liquid. For the smoothest results, purée in a high-speed food processor or blender. –J.S.

5 to 6 medium to large Yukon Gold potatoes, peeled

1 pound carrots, peeled

1 large white onion

1 eggplant, peeled

olive oil

salt and freshly ground black pepper, to taste

1 head garlic

1 to 2 quarts chicken broth

1 Parmesan cheese rind

2 bay leaves

1 tablespoon ground cumin, or to taste

1 cooked rotisserie chicken

heavy cream (optional)

Preheat oven to 400°F. Line one or two (depending on size) baking sheets with parchment paper.

Cut potatoes, carrots, onion, and eggplant into 1½- to 2-inch pieces. Place on baking sheet(s). Liberally sprinkle with olive oil and salt and pepper and toss to coat. Cut top off head of garlic and discard. Dot garlic with olive oil, wrap in aluminum foil, and add to prepared baking sheets. Bake for 1 hour, or until fork-tender, stirring occasionally.

Let the roasted vegetables cool slightly, then transfer to a stockpot. Squeeze the individual garlic cloves out of the head and add to stockpot. Cover vegetables with chicken broth and add Parmesan rind, bay leaves, and cumin. Simmer for 30 minutes. Remove Parmesan rind and bay leaves.

Remove meat from chicken and discard skin and bones. Cut into bite-size pieces.

Purée vegetables with chicken broth in batches.

Return to stockpot. Add about half of the chicken. Taste for seasoning and add salt, pepper, and cumin, as desired. Simmer again for 15 minutes. If soup is too thick, add more chicken broth or cream, to taste.

Makes 8 to 10 servings.

While making vegetable soup one day, I saw in my freezer the roasted eggplant that I had made the previous summer with eggplant from my garden. The idea to roast all my vegetables hit me. Root vegetables and eggplant might not be a conventional combination, but I sure like it! Some variations: Use other root vegetables, such as sweet potatoes or parsnips. Make it vegetarian with vegetable stock instead of chicken stock and leave out the chicken.

Ellen Elsbernd, Cincinnati, Ohio

SOUPS, CHOWDERS, & CHILIS

GRAMMA'S VEGETABLE BEEF SOUP

TESTER'S COMMENTS

An absolutely delicious, flavorful soup, loaded with vegetables. The chuck roast comes out nice and tender. I halved the recipe, and it made a very generous amount. I did not add salt because both the V8 and bouillon cubes contain it. –C.S.

½ cup vegetable oil

1 chuck roast (1 to 2 pounds)

salt and freshly ground black pepper, to taste

garlic powder, to taste

onion powder, to taste

6 beef bouillon cubes

2 cups diced onion

2 stalks celery, with leaves, diced

1 pound cabbage, chopped

1 can or bottle (46 ounces) regular V8 juice

2 cups peeled and diced potatoes

1 large carrot, diced

1 can (15.5 ounces) green beans, drained

1 can (15.5 ounces) baby green lima beans, drained

1 can (15.5 ounces) peas, drained

1 can (15.5 ounces) pinto beans, drained and rinsed

1 can (15.5 ounces) petite diced tomatoes, with juice

1 cup elbow macaroni

1 teaspoon salt, or to taste

½ teaspoon freshly ground black pepper, or to taste

1 can (15.5 ounces) corn, with liquid

I do this the same way every time, in the order listed. Any other way, and some vegetables will overcook.

Warm oil in a soup pot over medium-low heat. Season roast with salt and pepper, garlic powder, and onion powder. Add to pot and brown on all sides. Add water to just barely cover meat, about 4 cups. Add bouillon cubes and bring to a boil, cover, and simmer for 1 hour, or until meat is ready to fall apart. Transfer to a plate. Set aside to cool.

To broth, add onions, celery, cabbage, and V8 juice. Return to a boil, cover, and simmer for 45 minutes, or until cabbage is almost tender. Add potatoes, carrots, green beans, lima beans, peas, pinto beans, and tomatoes. Return to a boil, cover, and simmer for 15 minutes.

In a saucepan, cook macaroni according to package directions. Rinse under cool water and drain.

Cut meat into bite-size pieces.

Taste soup and add salt and pepper. Add corn, meat, and macaroni. Stir well. If it's too thick, thin with beef broth (1 cup hot water to 1 cube bouillon) and/or a few tablespoons of vegetable oil, and stir well.

Turn off heat and let rest for a few minutes. Stir well before serving.

To reheat leftovers, add more broth. (The veggies tend to soak up broth overnight in the fridge.)

Makes 12 or more servings.

I tried for years to replicate my grandmother's homemade vegetable soup recipe by how I remembered it looking and tasting. This is the end result. Family members agree that this is very close to Gramma's soup.

Rhonda Sine

❧ SLOW COOKER FRENCH ONION SOUP ☙

My husband and I love onion soup. We like to compare different restaurant versions. This is not like any other. It's a very good recipe and very easy to make. The idea of adding just a little cheese makes a big difference. –L.R.

½ cup (1 stick) butter or margarine

3 large onions, thinly sliced

4 cups hot water

2 tablespoons instant beef bouillon or 6 beef bouillon cubes

1 teaspoon Worcestershire sauce

½ teaspoon salt

4 slices toasted French bread

½ cup freshly grated Parmesan cheese

Melt butter in a skillet over low heat. Add onions and cook slowly, up to 45 minutes to release maximum flavor, or until nicely browned, stirring frequently. Transfer to a slow cooker. Add water, bouillon, Worcestershire sauce, and salt. Cover and cook on low for 4 to 6 hours.

To serve, top each bowl with 1 slice of bread. Sprinkle each with 2 tablespoons Parmesan. Recipe may be doubled and kept hot in slow cooker.

Makes 4 servings.

I developed this recipe by tinkering with four French onion soup recipes that I found in my cookbook collection, using as a base the ingredients and directions that occurred most often in the various recipes. I made it first for a church soup luncheon, then again for my elderly parents in Vermont, after my mother said that it was a favorite soup of hers and she hadn't had it in a long time. The joy of watching her eat that bowl of soup is with me to this day. It's not your usual French onion soup—there's no gooey cheese broiled over top—but it's a flavorful, easy recipe, made conveniently in a slow cooker. It's a keeper!

Daphne Turner, Slippery Rock, Pennsylvania

After peeling and cutting onions, rub salt on your wet
hands to get rid of the onion smell.

SOUPS, CHOWDERS, & CHILIS

❧ LAURA'S SOUP ❧

TESTER'S COMMENTS

This is a good soup, with lots of options for using leftovers or food on hand. Sample before serving and adjust seasonings. –L.R.

4 to 6 cups beef broth or water

6 large Roma tomatoes, diced, or 1 can (16 ounces) crushed tomatoes, with juice

2 pounds frozen mixed vegetables

1 cup frozen butter beans or baby limas

3 potatoes, cut into eighths

1 can (15.5 ounces) white corn, drained

1 to 2 tablespoons vegetable oil

1 to 1½ pounds ground beef, pork, turkey, or chicken

2 stalks celery, diced

1 onion, diced

¼ head cabbage, chopped

¼ teaspoon dried basil

¼ teaspoon dried oregano

¼ teaspoon dried marjoram

¼ teaspoon freshly ground black pepper

salt, to taste

Put 4 cups of broth into a soup pot and bring to a boil. Add tomatoes and cook for 10 minutes. Add frozen mixed vegetables, butter beans, and potatoes, cover pot, and cook for 20 minutes, or until soft. Add corn.

Heat 1 to 2 tablespoons oil in a skillet over medium heat. Add ground beef, celery, onions, cabbage, basil, oregano, marjoram, pepper, and salt. Cook, stirring, until meat is slightly browned. Add meat mixture to soup pot. Add water for thinner soup. For thicker, stewlike soup, add little or no water. Simmer for 10 to 15 minutes more, stirring occasionally. Serve with rice or with fried or baked corn bread or corn chips.

Makes 4 to 6 servings.

When my children were small, I worked very late. On grocery day, this is what we had. They loved it. Before my son passed away 20 years ago, he'd ask me to make this for him. I make it for my husband's friends sometimes now. I used to sell it. Those who bought it say that it is some of the best soup—or stew, when done as a stew—that they've ever had. Of course, I cook everything with an extra helping of love. That's what makes the difference! Fresh vegetables can be used, if desired; it will take longer to cook.

L. Jones-Hodge, Yuba City, California

SOUPS, CHOWDERS, & CHILIS

❧ OXTAIL SOUP ❧

Tasters found it hard to argue with tradition; they enjoyed every mouthful. The many flavors marry nicely to produce a tasteful broth and substantial soup; no single ingredient overwhelms the combination. Refrigerate the soup overnight and skim off the fat before serving. If time allows and to make a more pleasant experience for diners, before serving, take the meat from the bones and discard them. –C.S.

2 pounds oxtails

salt and freshly ground black pepper, to taste

1 tablespoon butter

1 tablespoon vegetable oil

1 onion, chopped

2 cloves garlic, minced

1 can (15 ounces) beef broth

1 head cabbage, chopped

3 carrots, diced

2 cans (14.5 ounces each) diced tomatoes, with juice

1 bay leaf

2 teaspoons dried parsley flakes

1 teaspoon dried thyme

Season oxtails with salt and pepper.

Heat butter and oil in a skillet over medium heat. Sear oxtails on all sides. Transfer to a slow cooker.

In the same skillet, cook onions and garlic until golden. Pour broth into skillet and deglaze it. Add to slow cooker with cabbage, carrots, tomatoes, bay leaf, parsley, and thyme. Cover and cook on high for 8 hours, or until vegetables are tender and meat easily pulls away from bones. Remove bay leaf before serving.

Makes 8 servings.

Soup recipes were an important part of my German mom's recipe collection. Cabbage was often used in her delicious soups. Oxtail soup, ochsenschwanzsuppe, *is a favorite family heirloom recipe.*

Bobbie Keefer, Byers, Colorado

Stock is made by simmering bones (or shells) and vegetables in water.
Broth is made by simmering meat and vegetables in water.

Canederli in Brodo (Italian Dumplings in Broth)

These are tasty when served warm in the broth—or eaten out of hand. I made 2-inch balls and boiled them for about 10 minutes. To make rolling the balls easier, first moisten your hands with water. –M.A.J.

1 Italian bread loaf (10 to 14 slices, crust removed, slightly dried)

1½ cups warm milk

8 slices bacon, finely chopped

1 onion, finely chopped

3 eggs, slightly beaten

½ pound Genoa salami or prosciutto, finely chopped

¼ cup grated Parmesan cheese

6 to 7 tablespoons finely chopped fresh parsley, divided

1 teaspoon salt

1 teaspoon freshly ground black pepper

¼ teaspoon nutmeg

½ to 1 cup all-purpose flour

chicken broth, heated

Moisten bread with milk. Squeeze out excess milk.

In a skillet over medium heat, cook bacon with onions for 5 to 8 minutes, or until bacon is crisp. Pour off and discard fat. Set pan aside to cool.

Bring a pot of water to a boil.

Mix together bread, onions and bacon, eggs, salami, Parmesan, 4 to 5 tablespoons parsley, salt, pepper, and nutmeg. Add enough flour to form soft balls about 3 inches in diameter. (You can make balls another size but must adjust cooking time.)

Drop balls, one at a time, into boiling water. Simmer 3-inch balls for 15 minutes, or until each puffs up and rises to the top. Remove balls carefully with a slotted spoon.

Serve one or two balls per bowl, covered with heated broth. Garnish with remaining parsley.

Makes 8 to 10 servings.

My mother came from a small mountain town in northern Italy, and this was a favorite of hers. She married my father, who came from the same town and they had 10 children. So this was a hearty, inexpensive soup for her family! I went to visit my Italian relatives, and they are still making and eating this soup many years later.

Ann Hicks, Indianapolis, Indiana

SOUPS, CHOWDERS, & CHILIS

❧ KIELBASA AND WHITE BEAN HOT POT ☙

TESTER'S COMMENTS

This was easy and quick to make and has good flavor. I served it with crusty French bread to my son and grandkids for dinner, and they all liked it. –M.A.J.

1 tablespoon butter

1 turkey kielbasa sausage (16 ounces), sliced into coins

2 cans (15.5 ounces each) cannellini beans, with liquid

1 can (14.5 ounces) diced fire-roasted tomatoes

1 tablespoon sugar, or to taste

½ teaspoon dried basil

salt and freshly ground black pepper, to taste

4 cups loosely packed fresh baby spinach

¼ cup grated Parmesan cheese, for topping

Melt butter in a soup pot over medium heat. Add kielbasa and brown on each side. Add beans, tomatoes, sugar, basil, and salt and pepper. Stir. Reduce heat and simmer for 10 minutes. Stir in spinach right before serving. Remove from heat. Pass Parmesan at the table.

Makes 4 servings.

This is a recipe that I created especially for my husband and two boys. It's warm and comforting—perfect for the many winter days that we have in Utah—but is very healthy, too. The wonderful broth for this dish tastes like it's been simmering all day, and the spinach adds freshness and brightness to the dish.

Shauna Havey, Roy, Utah

To store fresh spinach, dry off the leaves and put them
into a plastic bag. Refrigerate for up to 3 days.

SOUPS, CHOWDERS, & CHILIS

❧ LEMON PEPPER CHICKEN AND RICE SOUP ❧

TESTER'S COMMENTS

I like this soup very much. It's peppery-tasting. Others may also enjoy it more salted, too. One taster preferred more broth and less rice. Frozen peas or carrots, cooked, would stretch the dish further and add taste, noted another. For additional on-the-spot broth, I boiled the gizzards, neck, and liver with a couple of cups of water and added most of that to the bottom of the roaster when I roasted the chicken. –C.S.

4- to 5-pound chicken

olive oil

1 tablespoon lemon pepper seasoning, plus
     more to taste

chicken broth

1 cup rice

½ cup finely chopped celery (optional)

Preheat oven to 350°F.

Drizzle chicken with olive oil and sprinkle liberally with lemon pepper seasoning. Roast for 2 to 3 hours, or until done and juices run clear. Enjoy as dinner.

Place leftover chicken carcass in a soup pot. Add broth to cover. Bring to a boil, then simmer, covered, for 2 to 3 hours. Let cool. Remove carcass from soup pot, pull meat from bones, and discard bones.

Return meat to soup pot. Add lemon pepper seasoning and bring to a boil. Add rice and celery (if using). Cook until rice is done, about 30 minutes. Serve hot with rolls or crackers.

Makes 10 to 12 servings.

I was experimenting with stretching a chicken into multiple meals and with different flavors of roast chicken. We absolutely loved the lemon pepper version, but I wasn't sure how the next day's soup would turn out. I made the broth, added the rice, and then, on a whim, added the lemon pepper seasoning instead of salt. My daughter said at dinner that night, "This is the best soup I've ever had. It is now my favorite food on the planet." That was good enough for me.

Beverly Matoney, Johns Creek, Georgia

❧ BAKED FISH CHOWDER ❧

An outstanding recipe that's quick and easy because it's all made in the oven. There's no standing over a hot stove for this one. Celery lovers should add 1 rib, diced, to pan with seafood, onion, and liquids before baking. Thumbs up! —C.S.

---

1 pound haddock or cod, cut into bite-size pieces

1 pound scallops

3 cups diced, peeled potatoes or 8 small unpeeled red potatoes, diced

1 onion, sliced

¼ cup white wine

¼ cup (½ stick) butter

¼ cup all-purpose flour

2 cups light cream or milk

salt, to taste

freshly ground black pepper, to taste

garlic powder, to taste

Preheat oven to 350°F.

Combine fish, scallops, potatoes, onions, wine, and 2 cups water in a 13x9-inch baking dish. Cover with aluminum foil and bake for 30 minutes.

Melt butter in a saucepan. Stir in flour to make a roux. Add cream and stir until thickened. Add to baking dish. Add salt, pepper, and garlic powder. Cover and bake for 30 minutes more. Stir well before serving.

Makes 4 to 6 servings.

Almanac favorite

Be sure to smell scallops before buying; they should smell slightly sweet and not fishy.

Low Country Chowder

A chowder made from leftovers invites variations, which is always a convenience. Andouille sausage was handy; it worked fine and gave a lovely smoky flavor. Crab claws require steaming and provide big chunks of crab, but canned crab stood in nicely. Common seafood seasoning is Old Bay; 1 teaspoon, not ¼ teaspoon, was ideal for the tasters and me—probably because my ingredients were not the remains of a boil. –C.S.

2 tablespoons (¼ stick) butter

½ onion, chopped

1 cup sliced mushrooms

2 cloves garlic, minced

1 can (10.5 ounces) cream of mushroom soup

1 cup milk or half-and-half

1 teaspoon hot sauce

¼ teaspoon celery salt

¼ teaspoon Old Bay seasoning

salt and freshly ground black pepper, to taste

12 bite-size pieces kielbasa or smoked sausage

4 red potatoes, cooked and cut into quarters

4 to 6 crab claws or equivalent meat from body
   or 1 can (8 ounces) claw crabmeat (optional)

12 shrimp, cooked, peeled, and deveined

corn kernels from 2 cooked ears and scrapings
   from cobs

Melt butter in a soup pot over medium heat. Add onions, mushrooms, and garlic. Cook until onions are translucent. Add mushroom soup, milk, seasonings (generally go heavier on pepper), sausage, and potatoes. Cook on medium-low until well blended and small bubbles appear. Reduce heat to low and cook for 10 minutes. Add crab (if using), shrimp, and corn. Cook for a few minutes, or until heated through. Remove promptly from heat and serve.

Makes 4 servings.

My husband and I were raised near the coast and have always enjoyed Low Country boils. Almost always, there are a number of shrimp, some crab, some sausage, potatoes, and corn left over. These just don't taste as good cold, and trying to heat crab and shrimp by themselves is, um, well, kinda unappetizing. I hated throwing away the leftovers, so I made this chowder, and it is very tasty! If using ingredients from a boil, there is nice flavor from the seafood boil seasoning as well. You can adjust the amount of soup and milk (or half-and-half) to accommodate the amount of leftover boil ingredients, seasoning to taste before serving.

Michele Holloway, Augusta, Georgia

FIRE-BREATHING DRAGON CHILI

1½ teaspoons olive oil

2 stalks celery, diced

1 onion, diced

2 cloves garlic, minced

2 to 3 pounds ground sirloin beef

1 cup Bloody Mary bar mix

¼ cup vodka

1½ tablespoons chili powder

1 tablespoon ketchup

1 teaspoon ground cumin

1 teaspoon dried oregano

1 teaspoon McCormick's Montreal Steak seasoning

1 teaspoon Worcestershire sauce

1 teaspoon paprika

1 teaspoon Morton Nature's Seasons seasoning blend

1 teaspoon freshly ground black pepper

½ teaspoon Tabasco sauce

½ teaspoon crushed red pepper flakes

1 can (14.5 ounces) pinto beans, drained and rinsed

1 can (14.5 ounces) black beans, drained and rinsed if desired

1 can (14.5 ounces) red kidney beans, drained and rinsed if desired

In a skillet over medium heat, add enough oil to coat bottom. Add celery and onions and cook until translucent. Add garlic, stir, and add ground beef. Cook for 7 to 10 minutes, or until beef is browned. Drain off excess grease. Transfer mixture to a 6- or 7-quart slow cooker.

In a large pitcher, combine Bloody Mary mix, vodka, chili powder, ketchup, cumin, oregano, steak seasoning, Worcestershire sauce, paprika, seasoning blend, black pepper, Tabasco, and crushed red pepper flakes. Mix thoroughly.

Add beans to slow cooker. Pour Bloody Mary mixture over and stir to mix well. Cook on high for 4 hours or low for 8 hours.

Makes 7 to 8 servings.

A friend and I were drinking Bloody Marys after work one evening when we came to the realization that a Bloody Mary would taste great in chili. She suggested that I create a chili recipe using it. The Fire-Breathing Dragon Chili is it, and she and her husband and my husband love it. I even won a couple of chili cook-offs at work with this spicy chili recipe!

Brenda Whiteman, Springfield, Illinois

❧ NOT-TOO-SPICY VEGGIE AND LENTIL CHILI ❧

TESTER'S COMMENTS

I love one-pot soup recipes, and this is a keeper. The vegetable variety adds a lot of color and texture. Smoked paprika is undersung! If you have not tried it, do; it is dramatically different from Hungarian sweet–style. In a slow cooker, this cooked for about 4 hours on high. If you make it on a stovetop, sauté the onions in a bit of olive oil before adding other veggies and water. –D.T.

½ pound dried red or green lentils

4 to 5 carrots, diced

4 to 6 cloves garlic, minced

1 to 2 bell peppers, diced

1 red onion, chopped

1 cup diced tomatoes

1 cup fresh or frozen corn kernels

1 cup fresh or frozen shelled edamame

1 cup fresh or frozen chopped spinach

2 tablespoons apple cider vinegar

2 tablespoons smoked paprika

2 tablespoons dried parsley

2 teaspoons dried oregano

1 to 2 teaspoons cayenne pepper or 1 tablespoon hot sauce, or to taste

1 teaspoon dried thyme

1 teaspoon dried basil

1 teaspoon curry powder

1 vegan bouillon cube

salt and freshly ground black (or white) pepper, to taste

tahini, guacamole, and/or oyster crackers (optional toppings)

sour cream or cheese (nonvegan optional toppings)

Put all ingredients, except toppings, into an electric pressure cooker or slow cooker. Add enough water to cover.

For electric pressure cooker: Set for 11 minutes; let sit for 10 minutes after complete and then release valve.

For slow cooker: Cook on high for 2 to 3 hours or low for 6 to 8 hours.

Serve over rice or pasta or with baked potatoes or cornbread as a side.

Makes 6 servings.

I experimented with chili, soup, and stew recipes for a long time, trying to find a combination with a lot of vegetables that my husband (who is not overly fond of vegetables), my son (who doesn't like spicy food), and I (a vegan with celiac disease) would all enjoy. Ultimately, I found that none were satisfactory, but that if I took a few ingredients from each, I had a combination that we could all enjoy.

Erica Durian, DeKalb, Illinois

❧ Easy Bacon Sausage Chili

3 tablespoons olive oil

2 cloves garlic, minced

1 onion, diced

1 carrot, shredded

1 bell pepper, diced

1 pound ground beef

1 pound bacon sausage

1 jalapeño, stem removed, seeded, and finely diced

3 to 4 tablespoons masa (corn flour)

2 to 3 tablespoons chili powder

1 to 2 tablespoons paprika

1 to 2 teaspoons ground cumin

1 teaspoon dried oregano

½ teaspoon cayenne pepper

sriracha sauce, to taste

½ cup strong coffee

1 pip chocolate (from a Hershey bar)

1 can (15 ounces) diced tomatoes, with juice

1 can (15 ounces) tomato sauce

1 can (15 ounces) dark red kidney beans, drained and rinsed

1 can (15 ounces) light red kidney beans, drained and rinsed

1 can (15 ounces) cannellini (white) kidney beans, drained and rinsed

1 can (15 ounces) corn, drained

1 to 2 cups beef broth or water

salt and freshly ground black pepper, to taste

Heat olive oil in a soup pot over medium heat. Add garlic, onions, carrots, and bell peppers and cook until fragrant, or just translucent. Add beef and sausage and cook until browned. Add jalapeño, masa, chili powder, paprika, cumin, oregano, cayenne, and sriracha sauce and cook for 1 to 2 minutes. Add remaining ingredients and simmer for 20 to 30 minutes. Season with salt and pepper.

Makes 10 to 12 servings.

Warning!! This is a chili that many people can't stop eating. It has a perfectly sweet, spicy goodness. The shredded carrot adds flavor, sweetness, and texture.

James Magueflor, Palmer, Alaska

The heat of hot peppers is measured in what are called Scoville heat units (named for Wilbur Scoville, who developed the test). For example, a bell pepper measures in at zero Scoville heat units, but a habanero pepper has 100,000–350,000 Scoville heat units. Sriracha sauce comes in at 1,000–2,500 Scoville heat units.

❧ TURKEY CHILI ❧

3 cans (15 ounces each) dark red kidney beans, drained and rinsed

3 cans (15 ounces each) diced tomatoes, with juice

2 tablespoons chili powder

1 teaspoon salt

½ teaspoon freshly ground black pepper

2½ pounds ground turkey

2 to 3 tablespoons vegetable oil

2 to 3 onions, diced

In a soup pot over low heat, combine the beans and tomatoes. Add chili powder, salt, and pepper.

In a skillet, cook ground turkey until no longer pink. Add to soup pot.

Heat oil in same skillet. Add onions and cook until transparent. Transfer onions to soup pot. Add 1 cup water and stir. Cook until heated through.

Makes 12 servings.

This started out being my husband's recipe for chili, but, over the years, I started preparing it. I don't like hamburger because of the grease. So, I decided to try it with ground turkey. You can adjust your spices however you like it, but this is the way I prefer it.

Anna Garris, Webster, Kentucky

1 cup dried beans = about 2½ cups cooked beans
1 can (15 ounces) beans = about 1½ cups cooked dried beans

SOUPS, CHOWDERS, & CHILIS

❧ WHITE CHICKEN CHILI ❧

TESTER'S COMMENTS

This is different from my usual chili recipes. It's an excellent one. I'd make it again. –L.R.

2 pounds skinless chicken (1 pound bone-in thighs, 1 pound boneless breast)

2 large or 4 small chicken bouillon cubes

¼ cup (½ stick) butter

1 bunch celery, with leaves, finely diced

1 onion, finely diced

2 packages (1.25 ounces each) McCormick White Chicken Chili seasoning

1 can (15 ounces) black beans, drained and rinsed

1 can (15 ounces) navy beans, with liquid

1 can (15 ounces) great northern beans, with liquid

1 can (15 ounces) cannellini (white kidney) beans, with liquid

1 can (15 ounces) whole kernel corn, with liquid

1 can (12 ounces) evaporated milk

salt, to taste

sour cream, shredded cheddar cheese, chopped scallions, and/or cooked white rice, for garnish (optional)

tortilla chips (optional)

Place chicken in a 6-quart Dutch oven, add water to cover, and bouillon cubes. Simmer gently with lid askew for 1 hour, or until meat is falling off bones. Remove and let chicken cool. Strain and reserve stock.

Melt butter in a soup pot over low heat and add celery. Cook for 5 minutes. Add onions and cook for 5 minutes more. Add chili seasoning, stirring to dissolve. Cook for 2 minutes, then add reserved stock. Add black beans and simmer for 10 minutes.

Debone chicken and dice the meat.

Add navy, great northern, and cannellini beans to pot. Simmer for 5 minutes. Add diced chicken and corn and simmer for 5 minutes more. Add evaporated milk and ½ can water. Return to simmer; do not boil. Taste for seasoning and add salt.

If desired, serve topped with sour cream, shredded cheddar cheese, chopped scallions, and/or a scoop of white rice. Or serve with tortilla chips.

Makes 8 servings.

I saw the white chili seasoning packs in the store once several years ago and thought that they sounded interesting. I made it just as the package directed, and it was OK, but I thought that I could do better. A few more tries, and this was the end result. It's a big hit with everyone who eats it, and many people have requested this recipe over the years.

Rhonda Sine

MAIN DISHES

❧ BEEF IN A BED ❧

TESTER'S COMMENTS

This recipe is very easy and very good. Round it out with vegetables of your choosing, cooked separately. –M.S.

2 pounds sirloin steak tips
your favorite barbecue sauce or meat marinade
2 tablespoons (¼ stick) butter
10 ounces whole mushrooms
rice, your preference

The night before or in early morning of the day you want to serve it, cut sirloin tips into bite-size pieces. Transfer to a bowl, add sauce or marinade to cover, and stir to coat. Refrigerate until ready to cook.

In a skillet over low heat, melt butter, tilting to coat bottom. Add meat with sauce, cover, and cook for 20 to 30 minutes, turning occasionally.

Slice mushrooms to desired thickness. When meat is just about done, add mushrooms, and stir to combine. Cover, cook, and stir the mixture occasionally.

Prepare rice, according to package directions. Serve beef mixture over bed of rice.

Makes 4 servings.

I wanted barbecue sirloin tips, but wasn't quite sure how to cook them on the grill without charring them. I decided to cook them this way. All my ideas for dinners that are out of the ordinary come from when I shop hungry. This recipe is a family favorite and has now been handed down to my kids.

Vicki Fantozzi, Franklin, New Hampshire

Depending on where you live, sirloin steak tips
may be called flap meat, flap steak, loin tip steak, or bottom sirloin.

❧ SWISS BLISS ❧

TESTER'S COMMENTS

This is a hearty one-pot dish. If you prefer saucy stew, use a 28-ounce can of whole tomatoes instead of the 14.5-ounce one called for or add 1½ cups of beef broth. Cooking in foil makes for easy cleanup. If you do not want to turn on the oven, cook it in a slow cooker, on low for 8 hours. –M.A.J.

2 pounds 1-inch-thick chuck eye roast or chuck eye steak, cut into cubes

1 envelope (1 ounce) onion soup mix

½ pound mushrooms, sliced

½ green bell pepper, sliced

1 can (14.5 ounces) whole tomatoes, chopped and drained, with ½ cup juice reserved

½ onion, sliced

4 to 6 potatoes, peeled and quartered

¼ teaspoon salt

¼ teaspoon freshly ground black pepper

1 tablespoon A.1. Steak Sauce

1 tablespoon cornstarch

1 tablespoon chopped fresh parsley

Preheat oven to 375°F. Line a 13x9-inch baking dish with aluminum foil, with edges of foil extending over the sides enough to allow eventual closing. Spray foil with nonstick cooking spray.

Arrange meat cubes in baking pan, overlapping each piece. Sprinkle with dry soup mix, mushrooms, bell peppers, tomatoes, onions, potatoes, salt, and pepper.

Separately, mix reserved tomato juice with A.1. sauce and cornstarch. Pour over meat and vegetables. Fold aluminum foil over to enclose. Bake for 2 hours. Serve sprinkled with parsley.

Makes 4 servings.

I remember my mom making this dish quite often when my siblings and I were growing up; my dad was a big meat-and-potatoes guy. As kids, we thought it was neat to eat a meal from a big tinfoil pouch—really just an oven-baked stew. Although I have had the recipe for years (and I don't know where the name came from), I was so happy to find it in my mom's handwriting when we cleaned out my parents' home after she passed away in 2013. I cherish anything in her handwriting, especially her recipes. I think she would approve of me sharing it with everyone!

Kathy DeFranco, Queensbury, New York

❦ RIVERSSANCE STEW ❧

TESTER'S COMMENTS

The reader who contributed this recipe refers to a Welsh cawl. "Cawl" rhymes with "owl" and means, in Wales, a country soup made with the meats and vegetables that are seasonally available. This stew comes together more quickly than the ingredients list would have you think. Inspired by tradition, I cut up a top round steak instead of using stew meat; this saved cooking time and turned out really tender. –L.R.

4 to 5 tablespoons olive oil, divided

3 tablespoons chopped red onion

2 tablespoons chopped garlic

1 pound cubed beef steak

2 teaspoons salt, divided, plus more, to taste

½ teaspoon freshly ground black pepper, divided, plus more, to taste

1½ tablespoons butter

3 tablespoons all-purpose flour

2 teaspoons onion powder

2 teaspoons garlic powder

2 containers (16 ounces each) beef stock

3 tablespoons Worcestershire sauce

1 cup diced carrots

½ cup pearl barley

4 small red potatoes, cut into chunks

2 small rutabagas, peeled and diced

1 leek, diced

½ small head cabbage, shredded

Coat bottom of a stew pot with about half of the oil. Add onions and garlic. Cook until onions are almost transparent. Add beef cubes, 1 teaspoon salt, and ¼ teaspoon pepper and cook until beef is well browned. Add butter and remaining oil. After butter melts, sprinkle beef with flour, covering as much as possible. Add remaining salt and pepper plus onion powder and garlic powder and cook, stirring, for 2 minutes. Slowly and carefully add beef stock, stirring to avoid lumps. Add Worcestershire sauce and taste for seasonings. Add more salt and pepper, if desired.

When liquid base is well blended, add carrots, barley, potatoes, rutabagas, and leeks. Cover and simmer over medium heat, stirring occasionally and tasting to adjust seasonings.

When potatoes are almost done, add cabbage. Continue to simmer until potatoes and cabbage are tender.

Serve with crusty bread and fresh butter.

Makes 4 to 5 servings.

This is based on a Welsh cawl. I made it for the first meeting/potluck of the year for our Renaissance group (Riverssance!). Because we were meeting so close to St. Daffyd's Day (March 1; Daffyd is the patron saint of Wales), and the character I play is a Welsh duchess, it seemed fitting that this stew came to be.

Jean Gormally, Sioux City, Iowa

SLOW COOKER BEEF STROGANOFF

TESTER'S COMMENTS

This dish's flavor is excellent—and the tasters agreed: "We love the beef stroganoff—it was perfectly seasoned. The beef was incredibly tender and along with the onions and mushrooms made for a lovely dinner." –C.S.

2 tablespoons olive oil

2 to 3 pounds beef tips or chuck roast

1 pound mushrooms, sliced

1 onion, roughly chopped

3 cloves garlic, minced

1 cup red wine

1 tablespoon salt

1 teaspoon freshly ground black pepper

1 teaspoon ground coriander

1 container (16 ounces) sour cream

1 pound egg noodles

In a skillet over medium heat, warm oil. Add meat and cook until browned.

Transfer to a slow cooker. Add mushrooms, onions, garlic, wine, salt, pepper, and coriander, plus water to cover meat and vegetables. Cover and cook on high for 6 to 8 hours. Lift lid 30 minutes before it's done and add sour cream. Stir until mixture appears creamy.

Cook noodles according to package directions, or al dente. Add to slow cooker and stir.

Makes 6 to 8 servings.

My mom, the chef of the family, called me for this recipe while I was living in Virginia when my oldest son was small.

Kelly Baublitz, Rowlett, Texas

You can substitute grape or cranberry juice
for red wine in recipes. For an extra kick, add a tablespoon
of red-wine vinegar to the juice.

❦ SHEPHERD'S PIE ❧

Reader Joan (see below) is right. This is a tasty alternative to traditional shepherd's pie! –L.R.

1 pound ground beef

1 onion, chopped (optional)

1 can (10.5 ounces) cream of mushroom soup

1 cup canned or frozen and thawed vegetables (corn, peas, carrots, etc.)

½ cup milk

2 cups shredded cheese (your preference), divided

3 cups mashed potatoes

Preheat oven to 350°F.

In a skillet over medium heat, brown ground beef with onions (if using). Add soup, vegetables, and milk.

Transfer mixture to a 2-quart casserole. Sprinkle half of cheese on top. Layer mashed potatoes on cheese. Sprinkle with remaining cheese. Bake for 35 to 45 minutes, or until top is browned and edges are bubbling. Cool a bit before serving.

Makes 4 to 6 servings.

I started making this for my son, who just could not get enough of it. It is a great variation from the traditional shepherd's pie with gravy. Great for gifts and potlucks!

Joan Palmero, Coatesville, Pennsylvania

Originally, shepherd's pie was made with ground lamb.
If beef was used, it was called cottage pie.

MAIN DISHES: MEAT

❧ FABULOUS FLANK STEAK ❧

It took only minutes to get the flank steak into the slow cooker. Then, 7 hours later, this tough cut had cooked into a fork-tender piece of meat; no knives needed to serve or eat it. Cooked this way, flank is a good alternative to pot roast. Don't forget to make mashed potatoes to soak up the rich, dark juices. The pepper and heat are surprisingly mild. If you want the flavor to pop, add additional spices. –H.S.

1 tablespoon olive oil

1½ pounds flank steak, cut in half

1 onion, chopped in large chunks

2 to 4 cloves garlic

1 can (4 ounces) chopped green chiles, with juice

2 tablespoons white vinegar

1¼ teaspoons chili powder

1 teaspoon garlic powder

½ teaspoon honey

½ teaspoon salt

½ teaspoon freshly ground black pepper

In a skillet over medium heat, warm oil. Add steak and cook until browned. Transfer to a 5-quart slow cooker.

In the same skillet, cook onions for 1 minute. Gradually add ⅓ cup water, stirring to scrape up bits from bottom of skillet. If onions stick to the pan, add water before minute is up. Add garlic, green chiles, vinegar, chili powder, garlic powder, honey, salt, and pepper. Bring to a boil. Pour over steak. Cover and cook on low for 7 to 8 hours, or until meat is tender. (Check after 5 hours; add more water, if needed). Slice meat and serve with onions and pan juices.

Makes 4 to 6 servings.

This recipe was an accident. I'd never cooked flank steak and thought that I'd give it a try. I found a can of green chiles in the cupboard. Added the onions and garlic because I always add them to my stews. The vinegar was just a commonsense addition; it is a great tenderizer for tougher cuts of meat. It was a stroke of luck that it worked, but now it's one of my best dishes ever!

Camille Strate, Valley Center, California

GRANDMA'S MEATBALLS

½ pound 85% lean ground beef

½ pound ground pork

3 large eggs

6 cloves garlic, finely chopped

1 sweet onion, chopped

1 small red bell pepper, chopped

1 bunch Italian flat-leaf parsley, finely chopped

¾ cup freshly grated Pecorino Romano cheese

1 teaspoon kosher salt

1 teaspoon freshly ground black pepper

½ to 1 baguette (or loaf of French or Italian bread, no seeds)

olive oil for frying

In a bowl, combine all ingredients except bread and oil. Mix thoroughly.

Wet half of bread with water, then squeeze out excess water. Tear into small pieces and add to meat mixture. Mix with your hands. It should be sticky but hold together. If too wet (not holding together), wet remaining bread, squeeze out excess water, and add in pieces as necessary to make mixture sticky and hold together.

In a sauté pan or skillet over medium heat, warm 1 inch of olive oil until hot. Using ¼ cup of meat mixture at a time, form meatballs by hand or with an ice cream scoop. Add to oil (meatball should sizzle). Turn to brown on all sides. Drain meatballs on paper towels and serve with your favorite sauce.

Makes 25 to 35 meatballs.

All my life, I thought that these were my mother's meatballs. One afternoon, when I was actually making the recipe in front of her, she said, "Where did you learn how to make meatballs?" I said, "You taught me." She replied no, that it was not her recipe. "I don't put vegetables in, nor do I fry," she said. "I bake my meatballs." When I gave her a meatball out of the frying pan, she tasted it and said, "These are Grandma's meatballs!"—and we laughed. Enjoy!

Jo Ann Gallo, Bloomsbury, New Jersey

MAIN DISHES: MEAT

ℰ CELEBRATION MEATBALLS ℐ

TESTER'S COMMENTS

These meatballs are very good. Some tasters loved the sauce just the way it was, but others found it a little bit too tangy. To control flavor, start with less chili sauce and add more, to taste. –L.R.

1 pound ground chuck
½ cup bread crumbs
⅓ cup minced onions
¼ cup milk
1 egg
1 teaspoon chopped fresh parsley
1 teaspoon salt
⅛ teaspoon freshly ground black pepper
½ teaspoon Worcestershire sauce
¼ cup olive oil
1 jar (12 ounces) chili sauce
1 jar (10 ounces) grape jelly

In a bowl, combine all ingredients except oil, chili sauce, and grape jelly. Mix thoroughly. Shape into 1-inch balls.

In a skillet over medium-high heat, warm the oil. Add meatballs and brown on all sides. Drain meatballs on paper towels.

Pour off fat from skillet. Add chili sauce and grape jelly and cook over medium heat, stirring until jelly is melted. Return meatballs to pan and gently stir until thoroughly coated. Simmer uncovered for 30 minutes.

Makes 20 to 24 meatballs.

Many years ago, I went to a potluck. Someone made these and I fell in love with the flavor! I have made them many times and they are always a big hit! The mix of spicy and sweet makes my taste buds so happy! These meatballs have been there for many celebrations at my house, hence the name!

Chris Perez, Fresno, California

Ground chuck includes more fat and is more flavorful
than lean ground beef.

⚓ MEATBALLS WITH SAUCE ⚓

TESTER'S COMMENTS

An excellent dish. Pour the sauce over the meatballs for the last 15 minutes of cooking and serve warm to enhance the flavor. –M.S.

Meatballs:

1½ pounds 80% lean ground beef

¾ cup evaporated milk

1 cup quick-cooking oats

1 egg, beaten

½ cup chopped onion

1 teaspoon chili powder

½ teaspoon salt

½ teaspoon garlic salt, divided

¼ teaspoon freshly ground black pepper

Smoked barbecue sauce:

1 cup ketchup

1 cup packed dark-brown sugar

2 teaspoons liquid smoke

3 tablespoons dried minced onion

Preheat oven to 350°F.

For meatballs: In a bowl, combine ground beef, milk, oats, egg, onions, chili powder, salt, ¼ teaspoon garlic salt, and pepper and mix well. Form into about 24 meatballs. Place on a rimmed baking sheet. Bake for 35 to 40 minutes, or until browned.

For sauce: In another bowl, combine ketchup, brown sugar, liquid smoke, dried minced onions, and remaining garlic salt and stir to blend. Pour over hot meatballs and serve.

Makes about 24 meatballs.

Our family enjoys these meatballs. They are really good to take to family reunions. My family expects me to make these every year.
Richard Miller

To make meatballs or meat loaf gluten-free, use oatmeal
instead of bread crumbs as the binder.

❧ Aunt Barb's Special Meatball Sauce ❧

This was delicious and is infinitely customizable. It's a mild sauce that can be made spicier by reducing the honey and adding one or two crushed garlic cloves and hot sauce or chili powder. Or use a spicier salsa. Red-wine vinegar can stand in for pomegranate juice (not available to me). Instead of meatballs, I poured it over slices of tempeh and baked in a covered dish for 30 minutes at 325°F. I also used it with veggie burgers and baked beans. As the saying goes, you can have it your way! –D.T.

1 can (12 ounces) tomato paste

1 cup mild or medium salsa, drained

1 cup honey

½ cup ketchup

2 tablespoons packed brown sugar

1 to 2 tablespoons barbecue sauce

2 teaspoons soy sauce

1 teaspoon spicy prepared mustard
(such as Dijon-style)

1 teaspoon pomegranate juice

½ to 1 teaspoon seasoned salt (see below)

freshly ground black pepper, to taste

In a bowl, combine all ingredients and mix until brown sugar dissolves.

Pour over uncooked meatballs, franks, or ribs—any meat.

If using a slow cooker, cook on low for 4 hours or on high for 2 hours. Stir occasionally.

If using an oven, preheat to 200°F. Bake for 1 to 2 hours, or until meat is heated and/or cooked through.

Makes 10 to 12 servings and can be easily doubled.

This sauce was born out of boredom and cooking in winter when there are fewer fresh foods available. I put it on meat loaf and it was fantastic! The name comes from my nieces and nephews and great-nieces and -nephews always wondering what I'm "cooking up."

Barbara Ross, Hagerstown, Maryland

HOW TO MAKE SEASONED SALT
Combine ½ teaspoon salt with a dash each of
cayenne, chili powder, garlic powder, mustard powder,
allspice, and freshly ground black pepper.

❦ MEAT LOAF ❧

Ketchup lovers will go for this; it uses a lot (cut back, if you like). The mustard and brown sugar help to balance the flavors. The ingredients create a delicious aroma while this excellent meat loaf is in the oven. –C.S.

1½ pounds ground beef

1 cup seasoned bread crumbs

1 onion, diced

1 bell pepper, diced

2 eggs, beaten

1½ cups ketchup

⅓ cup prepared mustard

⅓ cup packed brown sugar

1 tablespoon apple cider vinegar

Preheat oven to 400°F.

In a bowl, mix together ground beef and bread crumbs. Mix in onions and bell peppers. Add eggs and mix to combine.

In a 13x9-inch baking dish, shape mixture into a loaf.

In another bowl, combine ketchup, mustard, brown sugar, and vinegar. Pour over loaf. Bake for 40 minutes, or until done.

Makes 6 servings.

My family loves it!!
Carole Lawson, Bowdon, Georgia

A "free-form" meat loaf will have a crispy exterior and moist interior.
It will also cook faster and more evenly.

❦ INDIAN SUMMER SLIDERS ❧

6 slices Applewood smoked bacon

Relish:
3 tablespoons butter
2 Gala apples, peeled, cored, and finely diced
1 yellow onion, finely diced
1 teaspoon chili paste or sambal oelek (near hot sauces in most large supermarkets)
½ teaspoon kosher salt

Mayonnaise:
1 lemon
½ cup mayonnaise
2 tablespoons thinly sliced scallions

Sliders:
2 pounds freshly ground beef chuck
¼ cup finely chopped fresh Italian parsley
2 teaspoons salt
1 tablespoon Worcestershire sauce
1 tablespoon Balsamic Glaze (see page 128)
1 tablespoon melted butter
2 teaspoons dark-brown sugar
1 teaspoon chili paste
12 slices sharp white cheddar cheese

12 brioche slider rolls or dinner rolls, split in half
1 cup coarsely chopped red leaf lettuce

Preheat oven to 400°F. Line a rimmed baking sheet with aluminum foil. Preheat grill to medium-high.

Arrange bacon in single layer on baking sheet. Cook in oven for 10 to 12 minutes, or until brown and crispy.

For relish: In a skillet over medium heat, melt butter. Add apples and onions and cook for 5 to 10 minutes, or until tender. Add chili paste and salt. Remove from heat and cover to keep warm.

For mayonnaise: Remove zest from lemon and set aside. Juice half of lemon. In a bowl, combine zest and lemon juice. Add mayonnaise and scallions and stir to combine.

For sliders: Break beef into clumps by hand and put into a bowl. Add parsley and salt.

In another bowl, whisk together Worcestershire sauce, Balsamic Glaze, melted butter, brown sugar, and chili paste.

Add to beef and gently mix to combine. Form into 12 patties.

(continued on page 128)

MAIN DISHES: MEAT

Cook on grill for 3 minutes. Turn over, top each with slice of cheddar, and cook for 3 minutes more. Transfer patties to a plate.

Place rolls split side down on grill for 1 minute, or until lightly toasted.

To assemble: Spread mayonnaise on bottom half of each roll. Arrange lettuce on top. Add patty, cheese side up. Halve each bacon slice. Put one half on each patty. Top with relish and remaining roll halves.

Makes 12 sliders.

These fall-theme sliders are inspired by that unexpected heat that sometimes surprises us in the early fall in New England. The sweet-and-savory topping is made with crisp Gala apples that our local orchards overflow with each fall. The secret ingredient for these scrumptious sliders, however, is the chili paste that gives them a burst of unexpected heat.

Veronica Callaghan, Glastonbury, Connecticut

HOW TO MAKE BALSAMIC GLAZE

In a saucepan over medium heat, combine 1 cup balsamic vinegar
with ¼ cup brown sugar. Allow sugar to melt, then bring
to a low boil and cook for 2 minutes, or until glaze coats the back of a spoon.
Cool, transfer to a jar with a lid, and keep in the refrigerator.

BRAISED OXTAILS

TESTER'S COMMENTS

Tasters were over the Moon: "I loved the sweet rich flavors and velvet texture of the meat" and "WOW! What is that flavor?"—the latter from a man whose family has oxtails with black-eyed peas every New Year's Day for luck. Knowing oxtails to be fatty, he suggested pan braising them in butter or light oil, yet praised the sweet reduction and succulent meat. On another note: Check the liquid after 1 hour in the oven; if the liquid is evaporating, add more and reduce heat by 25°F. –C.S.

4 pounds oxtails

2 tablespoons clarified butter (see below) or animal fat (e.g., bacon, beef, or duck fat)

3 stalks celery, diced

2 carrots, diced

1 onion, diced

2 to 4 large cloves garlic, minced

1 tablespoon Thai fish sauce

½ cup coconut aminos or soy sauce

2 bay leaves

2 teaspoons dried thyme

2 teaspoons freshly ground black pepper

approximately 2 quarts water or chicken or beef stock

Preheat oven to 350°F.

In a Dutch oven or heavy pot, brown oxtails in clarified butter. Remove and set aside.

In the same pot, sauté celery, carrots, and onions. Add garlic in final moments so that it does not scorch. When onions are soft, add fish sauce and coconut aminos and cook, scraping up brown bits from bottom of pot. Return oxtails to pot and turn off heat. Add bay leaves, thyme, pepper, and enough water to reach bottom third of oxtails. Do not overfill. Cover and bake for 2½ to 3 hours, or until meat is falling off bones. Remove bay leaves before serving.

Makes 6 to 8 servings.

My husband and I are building a farm, so after being a city girl for 40-something years, I decided that it was time for me to finally learn to cook since we'll be growing our own food now. I started braising this dish stovetop-style in a travel trailer with only a cooktop, during the building of our "barndominium." The dish would occasionally stick, and fussing over the level of liquid was a huge chore. Now that we have a fabulous kitchen and six-burner gas stove, it's a breeze braising in the oven. The gravy makes itself from the slow cooking and tough pieces of meat. This is southern comfort food at its best.

Karyn Medders, Grapeland, Texas

HOW TO MAKE CLARIFIED BUTTER

In a saucepan over medium heat, melt butter. When completely melted, reduce heat to low. Allow butter to boil gently until it reaches 260°F and the foam on top is slightly browned. Pour into a container through cheesecloth and discard solids.

❧ Texas Tamale Pie ❧

A tasty and hearty dish, this is even better on the second day, when the flavors have had time to "marry." –C.S.

Filling:

1 tablespoon butter

1 onion, chopped

1 green bell pepper, diced

¾ pound ground beef

2 cups tomato sauce

¾ cup canned or frozen whole-kernel corn

½ cup ripe olives, chopped

1 clove garlic, minced

1 tablespoon sugar (optional)

1½ teaspoons chili powder

1 teaspoon salt

½ teaspoon freshly ground black pepper

1 cup shredded Monterey Jack cheese

Topping:

2 cups cold water

¾ cup cornmeal

½ teaspoon salt

1 tablespoon butter

Preheat oven to 375°F. Grease an 8x8-inch or 10x6-inch baking dish.

For filling: In a skillet over medium heat, melt butter. Add onions and bell peppers and cook until tender. Add meat and cook until browned. Stir in tomato sauce, corn, olives, garlic, sugar (if using), chili powder, salt, and pepper. Simmer for 20 minutes. Add cheese and stir until melted. Pour into prepared baking dish and set aside.

For topping: Pour water into a saucepan, add cornmeal and salt, and stir. Cook over medium heat, stirring, until thickened. Stir in butter.

Spoon generous dollops of topping over meat mixture. Bake for 40 minutes, or until bubbly hot.

Makes 6 servings.

Almanac favorite

MAIN DISHES: MEAT

Unrolled Cabbage Roll-ups

I grew up eating stuffed cabbage rolls (we called it "pig in a blanket"), and the flavors of the traditional dish as I know it are replicated here wonderfully. This recipe halves easily for a smaller quantity. –C.S.

2½ to 3 pounds lean ground beef

1 onion, chopped

2 eggs

¾ cup ketchup

½ cup cooked rice

½ cup bread crumbs, seasoned or unseasoned

2 teaspoons Worcestershire sauce

1 medium to large cabbage, chopped

2 cans (10.5 ounces each) condensed tomato soup

1 can (14.5 ounces) diced tomatoes, with juice

1 can (14.5 ounces) stewed tomatoes, with juice

mashed potatoes (optional)

Preheat oven to 350°F. Use a roasting pan with high lid (such as a turkey roaster) or see tip below for alternative.

In a bowl, combine ground beef, onions, eggs, ketchup, rice, bread crumbs, and Worcestershire sauce and mix to blend. Shape into loaf and place in roasting pan. Spread chopped cabbage around and over loaf. (Cabbage will cook down.)

In another bowl, mix together tomato soup, 1½ cans water, and diced and stewed tomatoes. Pour over cabbage and meat. Cover with lid. Bake for 3 to 3½ hours, or until cabbage is tender, stirring cabbage gently halfway through. Serve over mashed potatoes, if desired.

Makes 6 to 8 servings.

I come from a large family, and sometimes there just was not time to put together a recipe the way it should be done, e.g., cabbage roll-ups. When I was in high school, I experimented and found that making one big loaf saves time and tastes exactly as meat rolled in individual cabbage leaves. My mom was not always happy about it, but she could see how it saved time.

Christine Strainer, New Market, Tennessee

HOW TO MAKE A ROASTER PAN

The reason for the high-top roaster is to let the cabbage and tomato mixture steam undisturbed, except for stirring halfway through. You can improvise by using a shallow aluminum pan (13x9 inches, with 3-inch-high sides) topped by a 9x8-inch aluminum pan with 4½-inch sides. Seal the edges with crimped aluminum foil, then poke four vent holes in the "lid." Support the bottom pan with a baking sheet. Undo the foil to check and stir the dish halfway through.

❧ STUFFED ACORN SQUASH ❧

This recipe is easy and delicious. My husband and I had it for supper, and it made plenty. So simple and original! –L.R.

1 large acorn squash, halved and seeded
olive oil, to taste
salt and freshly ground black pepper, to taste
1 pound ground sausage
1 apple or pear, cored and diced

Preheat oven to 400°F. Line a baking sheet with aluminum foil.

Place squash, cut side up, on prepared baking sheet. Drizzle with olive oil and sprinkle with salt and pepper. Bake for 30 to 45 minutes, or until flesh is tender.

In a skillet over medium heat, brown sausage. When cooked thoroughly, add apples and stir until fruit is softened. Season with salt and pepper.

Stuff cooked squash cavity with sausage mixture. Bake for 10 to 15 minutes more. Cool slightly before serving.

Makes 2 servings.

One cold and rainy night, my husband and I were feeling lazy but wanted something healthy to eat. I was determined to create a dish that we would both love and want again. This is a staple for us now!

Anna Green, Pearland, Texas

If using small acorn squash, cut 1 to 2 inches
off the top and scoop out the seeds. To make the squash
stand upright, cut off a slice from the bottom.

MAIN DISHES: MEAT

BAKED HAM

What a delicious way to dress up plain old ham! Testers practically licked their plates clean. –S.L.P.

1 ham
1 bottle (12 ounces) beer, divided
½ cup packed brown sugar
3 tablespoons honey mustard

Preheat oven to 300°F.

Put ham in a roaster pan. Pour 1¼ cups of beer over ham. Cover. Roast according to package directions.

In a bowl, combine brown sugar, honey mustard, and remaining beer. About 30 minutes before ham finishes cooking and every 10 minutes thereafter, spread one-third of glaze on ham. Remove ham from oven. Let rest for 10 to 15 minutes before carving.

Ever since my sister got this ham recipe from a college classmate, it has been the one my family has used.
Cynthia Schlosser, Peterborough, New Hampshire

A ham glaze is usually sweet in order to contrast the saltiness of the ham. The glaze can be made with brown sugar, honey, maple syrup, jam, marmalade, or fruit.

BAKED PINEAPPLE DRESSING

An excellent accompaniment to baked ham. –J.S.

2 eggs

1 can (20 ounces) crushed pineapple, with juice

¾ cup sugar

3 tablespoons cornstarch

½ teaspoon salt

1 teaspoon ground cinnamon

2 teaspoons (¼ stick) butter

Preheat oven to 350°F. Grease a 2-quart casserole.

In a bowl, beat eggs slightly. Add pineapple, sugar, cornstarch, and salt. Stir to combine thoroughly.

Pour mixture into prepared casserole. Sprinkle with cinnamon and dot with butter. Cover with lid or aluminum foil. Bake for 1 hour, 15 minutes. Do not stir.

Makes 6 to 8 servings.

My Aunt Agnes brought this Virginia recipe into our family. She and my Uncle Carl were married after having met on a blind date when he was stationed at Fort Pickett, Blackstone, Virginia. It is a simple recipe, but one that always had a place on the table with a baked ham when Mother's family gathered for celebrations or family picnics. Mom always makes it when she serves pork chops for Sunday dinner. It's a nice change from applesauce.

Cynthia Schlosser, Peterborough, New Hampshire

All out of cornstarch? Use arrowroot or potato starch instead. Or use tapioca flour (2 tablespoons for every 1 tablespoon of cornstarch).

❦ Ham Yam Ramekins ❧

I love the individual ramekin servings, and I think that's the key to maintaining this dish's strong flavors. We regretted not having more than 2 days' worth of leftovers! –M.S.

2 to 3 yams or 2 cups drained and mashed canned yams

1 cup warm milk, divided

2 tablespoons (¼ stick) butter

½ cup diced green bell pepper

1 can (10.5 ounces) cream of mushroom soup

1 tablespoon Dijon-style mustard

1 tablespoon grated onion

freshly ground black pepper, to taste

¼ cup cold water

3 tablespoons all-purpose flour

3 cups cooked and diced ham

pineapple and marshmallow pieces, for topping

Preheat oven to 350°F. Butter six ramekins.

Peel, slice, and boil yams until tender. Drain, mash to make 2 cups, and place in a bowl. Add ⅓ cup warm milk and beat until fluffy.

In a skillet over medium heat, melt butter. Add bell peppers and cook for 8 minutes, or until soft.

In a saucepan, combine soup and remaining milk. Add mustard, onions, and black pepper.

In a bowl, blend together water and flour. Add to soup mixture and stir over low heat until thickened. Add bell peppers and ham and stir to coat.

Divide ham mixture among prepared ramekins. Top each with mashed yams and top with pineapples and marshmallows. Bake for 20 to 25 minutes.

Makes 6 servings.

Almanac favorite

If you don't have ramekins, you can use oven-safe coffee cups or mugs.

MAIN DISHES: MEAT

❧ HAM SALAD ❧

TESTER'S COMMENTS

Dill pickles provide a tasty alternative to the "regular" version that uses sweet relish. Duke's mayonnaise was not available, so I used Hellmann's instead. This recipe made me long for a grocery-shopping trip down South. –L.R.

1 package (16 ounces) diced cooked ham

1 yellow onion, finely diced

1 jalapeño pepper, ribs and seeds removed (unless you prefer extra heat) and finely diced

2 tablespoons finely diced dill pickle

¼ cup mayonnaise (preferably Duke's)

¼ teaspoon salt

freshly ground black pepper, to taste

Put ham into a saucepan, cover with water, and boil for 30 minutes (boiling improves texture of precooked ham). Drain, cool briefly, then transfer to a food processor. Pulse six to eight times.

In a bowl, combine onions, peppers, and pickles. Add ham, mayonnaise, salt, and pepper and mix until combined. Serve as sandwich spread or dip.

Makes 4 to 6 servings.

Great recipe for leftover holiday baked ham.
Julia Jordan, Lake Wylie, South Carolina

To stretch ham salad a bit further, add two finely chopped boiled eggs. Many cooks also add a teaspoon or two of spicy mustard for extra flavor.

❧ ROCKY MOUNTAIN CUBAN PORK ❧

This is cooked on the stovetop and requires some attention, but you will be rewarded: It is absolutely delicious. The meat is tender and the thickened citrus sauce wonderful. Every taster had seconds. –M.A.J.

½ cup extra-virgin olive oil, divided

2 pounds lean pork loin, cut into 4 to 6 pieces

4 cups orange juice, divided

1 cup fresh lemon juice, divided

4 cloves garlic, minced

1 teaspoon ground cumin

salt and freshly ground black pepper, to taste

black beans and rice (optional)

In a skillet over medium-high heat, warm 1 tablespoon oil. Add pork and sear.

In a bowl, combine ¼ cup oil, 1 cup orange juice, and ¼ cup lemon juice. Set aside.

When meat is browned, reduce heat to medium. Add garlic, cumin, and salt and pepper. Cook for about 30 seconds. Do not burn garlic. Slowly pour in orange juice mixture. Baste meat with a spoon. Continue basting every 15 minutes for 1 hour. When liquid is reduced and thickened, add remaining oil, 1 cup orange juice, and ¼ cup lemon juice. Continue basting every 15 minutes until pork is tender, adding remaining orange and lemon juices as needed when liquid reduces. Serve with black beans and rice, if desired.

Makes 4 to 6 servings.

Tampa Bay has a rich Cuban history, and Cuban cuisine was always on the menu at our house. Yellow rice and chicken (arroz con pollo), *plantains* (plantanos) *fried in butter, and black beans and rice* (frijoles negros con arroz) *were weekly staples. However, my daughter's favorite dish has always been Cuban pork, made with sour orange juice. We had sour orange trees growing in our yard, and we shared the fruit with family and friends, as they were difficult to find in local stores. When my daughter and her husband moved to Colorado, she missed the food that she grew up on in Florida. Since there was no way to get sour oranges in Colorado, she developed this recipe, which is almost identical in flavor to the original.*

Barbara Vogel, Gibsonton, Florida

MAIN DISHES: MEAT

❧ Sweet Tea–Peach Low Country Pork Ribs

TESTER'S COMMENTS

A delicious, satisfying dish that will feed a crowd! The pork ribs get better the longer they cook, which for me was 8 hours on low. They were tender and had a citrusy, spicy taste. For the sweet tea, I used a cup of brewed, black breakfast tea with 1 tablespoon of sugar mixed in. It was too early for fresh peaches, so instead I used a 16-ounce bag of frozen peach slices, thawed. The rice mixed with toasted pecans was the perfect accompaniment. –M.A.J.

3 pounds boneless country-style pork ribs

3 fresh peaches, peeled, pitted, and sliced

1 sweet onion, thinly sliced

1 lemon, halved and seeded

1 cup sweet tea

1 teaspoon ground cinnamon

½ teaspoon ground ginger

½ teaspoon salt

¼ teaspoon freshly ground black pepper

⅛ teaspoon ground cloves

4½ cups hot cooked rice pilaf

¼ cup toasted pecans

Place all ingredients, except rice and pecans, in a 5-quart slow cooker. Stir to coat. Cover and cook on low for 7 to 9 hours.

In a bowl, stir together rice and pecans. Drizzle with juices from slow cooker and serve alongside pork.

Makes 6 servings.

My grandma's family lived in the South, but I was raised in northern Minnesota. While serving in the U.S. Navy, I spent a good bit of time in Georgia, South Carolina, and Tennessee, where I developed a love of southern cuisine. My grandmother was a great cook and used whatever she had on hand. I based this recipe on a dish she used to make and added a few of my own touches. I think Grandma would approve!

Crystal Schlueter, Northglenn, Colorado

Country-style ribs are the meatiest variety.
They are cut from the sirloin or rib end of the pork loin.

MAIN DISHES: MEAT

EASY DUTCH OVEN COUNTRY RIBS

TESTER'S COMMENTS

My son and a friend stopped by the night I made these ribs, and they tried some. They loved the sweet and spicy flavor. My son's friend actually texted me the next day asking if I could share the recipe with his wife! —M.S.

Rub:

2 tablespoons freshly ground black pepper

2 tablespoons garlic powder

1 tablespoon onion powder

1 tablespoon guajillo chili powder or ancho powder

1 tablespoon kosher salt

1 teaspoon cayenne pepper

6 country-style ribs

Sauce:

1 cup ketchup

¼ cup dark beer or Coca-Cola

2 tablespoons chopped garlic

2 tablespoons honey

2 tablespoons molasses

1 tablespoon olive oil

1 yellow onion, chopped

1 cup dark beer or Coca-Cola

2 teaspoons non-MSG chicken base

For rub: Combine black pepper, garlic powder, onion powder, chili powder, salt, and cayenne. Mix thoroughly with a fork. Rub ribs with mixture, place in a plastic bag, seal, and refrigerate for 2 to 3 hours.

Preheat oven to 225°F.

For sauce: In a container with lid, mix ketchup, beer, garlic, honey, and molasses. Seal and refrigerate.

Warm oil in a Dutch oven over medium heat. Add ribs and brown on all sides. Add chopped onions.

In a bowl, combine beer and chicken base. Add to ribs and stir. Cover and bake for 6 hours. Remove and discard all fat and liquid. Brush sauce onto ribs. Return to oven uncovered and cook for 1 hour more.

Makes 3 servings.

I like beer, so . . .

Jeff Porter, Milwaukee, Wisconsin

Pop's Barbecue Sauce

Never before had I made barbecue sauce, and this I *will* make again! The peppers and onions make it chunky. My family loved it on burgers. –L.R.

½ cup chopped red onion

½ cup chopped green bell pepper

⅓ cup sweet pickle relish

½ cup ketchup

⅓ cup apple cider vinegar

3 tablespoons brown sugar

2 teaspoons prepared mustard

1 teaspoon salt

½ teaspoon freshly ground black pepper

In a saucepan over medium heat, combine onions, bell peppers, relish, and ketchup. Cook for 1 minute, stirring constantly. Add vinegar, brown sugar, mustard, salt, and pepper and heat to boiling. Boil for 5 minutes, then reduce to simmer. Cook until sauce is thick and onions and peppers are tender.

Makes ¾ cup to 1 pint.

This is a favorite sauce that my father used to make.

Alan McMunn, Davenport, Iowa

Chopped vegetables make a coarse-texture barbecue sauce.
If you prefer a smooth sauce, purée the vegetables in a food processor.

MAIN DISHES: MEAT

PORK AND APPLES WITH RED CABBAGE

This classic fall recipe is as pretty as it is flavorful. —S.L.P.

2 tart apples, peeled, cored, and sliced

2 teaspoons fresh lemon juice

5 tablespoons vegetable oil, divided

1 pound boneless pork tenderloin, cut into thin strips

2 onions, thinly sliced

1 small head red cabbage, finely shredded

1 cup unsweetened apple juice

¼ cup red currant jelly

3 tablespoons red-wine vinegar

¼ teaspoon allspice

salt and freshly ground black pepper, to taste

In a bowl, toss apples with lemon juice and set aside.

In a heavy skillet over medium heat, warm 3 tablespoons of oil. Brown pork, then remove to paper towels to drain.

Add remaining 2 tablespoons of oil to skillet. Add onions and cook until soft but not brown. Add cabbage and cook, stirring often, until cabbage begins to wilt. Add apples and pork and stir well.

In another bowl, combine apple juice, jelly, vinegar, allspice, and salt and pepper. Pour over cabbage and pork, stirring to coat evenly. Reduce heat to medium-low, cover skillet tightly, and simmer for 10 to 15 minutes. Check occasionally, adding water if skillet gets dry.

Makes 4 servings.

Almanac favorite

Red cabbage is higher in fiber, vitamins A and C, calcium, iron, and potassium than green cabbage.

❧ SOUVLAKI SANDWICH ❧

My butcher kindly cut a lamb steak for me to use since stew meat was not available. After having been marinated and then grilled to medium rare, the lamb was mouthwateringly wonderful. –C.S.

Meat:

1 pound lamb kabobs (stew meat)

1 cup olive oil

2 tablespoons lemon juice

1 tablespoon dried oregano

½ teaspoon salt

Dressing:

5 cloves garlic, chopped

1 cup olive oil

2 tablespoons lemon juice

2 tablespoons crumbled feta cheese, or to taste

1 tablespoon balsamic vinegar

1 tablespoon chopped fresh oregano

¼ teaspoon salt

4 or 5 pita bread rounds

1 large white onion, sliced and cut into half- or quarter-rings

2 large tomatoes, chopped

1 cup crumbled feta cheese

If using wooden skewers, soak them overnight to prevent flaming on the grill.

For meat: Skewer 5 or 6 pieces of lamb onto each of several skewers.

In a bowl, combine olive oil, lemon juice, oregano, and salt. Pour into a shallow baking dish. Lay lamb skewers in dish, turning to cover all sides. Cover and marinate in refrigerator at least 4 hours or overnight.

Discard marinade. Grill lamb over coals or broil in oven until medium-rare or medium. (Lamb cooked "well" will be tough.)

For dressing: In a bowl, combine garlic, olive oil, lemon juice, feta, vinegar, oregano, and salt. Stir to blend.

To assemble: Cut pitas in half or cut off top third of pita. Put one skewer of lamb into each pita. Add onions, tomatoes, and feta. Add dressing, to taste. Best if all used after 1 day.

Makes 4 or 5 servings.

This is my family's favorite dish and was re-created from a local restaurant. Later, when I moved away from home, I never could get it right . . . until I made it with lamb one day and voilà: *that was the key ingredient. I had been using sirloin beef. Don't skimp on the lamb; preferably, use organic, grass-fed lamb. (We raise our own just for this dish.) You will crave this meal after eating it just once.*

Cheryl Franklin, Goodman, Missouri

YANKEE CHICKEN CORDON BLEU

Few three-ingredient dishes taste this good. I liked this more than I thought I would! The only change I made was to sprinkle seasonings (salt, pepper, garlic, and oregano) on chicken after rolling up. –M.S.

4 boneless, skinless chicken breast halves

4 slices bacon

1 package (8 ounces) cream cheese with chives

Preheat oven to 350°F. Lightly coat bottom of a 13x9-inch baking dish with nonstick spray.

Pound chicken breasts to uniform thickness.

Cut cream cheese into four pieces. Place one on each breast, then roll up chicken, keeping cream cheese inside. Wrap a slice of bacon around each breast. Secure with toothpicks, if desired. (Remove toothpicks before serving.)

Place wrapped breasts in prepared baking dish. Bake for 45 minutes, or until chicken is firm, juicy, and no longer pink.

Makes 4 servings.

I serve this with chicken-flavor cream sauce and stuffing or mashed potatoes. My family loves it! I watched my mother-in-law make this because my husband loved it. I was married at 19 and wanted to impress him. He finally says I'm as good as his mom, who was an exceptional cook! We've been married for almost 33 years. Goal achieved, I guess!

Evelyn Pendleton, Webster, New Hampshire

There is a noble history behind the name "cordon bleu"
(French for "blue ribbon"), dating back to the French Order of St. Esprit in 1578.
However, the chicken dish likely originated in mid–20th century America:
The first known mention was in 1967, in *The New York Times*.

MAIN DISHES: POULTRY

CRISPY BUTTERMILK CHICKEN TENDERS WITH TANGY BUTTERMILK DIPPING SAUCE

Marinating the chicken in buttermilk makes it wonderfully moist, and the dipping sauce is a nice change from traditional honey mustard. –S.L.P.

Sauce:

¾ cup feta cheese, crumbled

½ cup buttermilk

½ cup sour cream

1 tablespoon finely chopped fresh parsley

¼ teaspoon freshly ground black pepper

2 scallions (green part only), thinly sliced

1 clove garlic, minced

Chicken:

1 cup buttermilk

1 pound boneless, skinless chicken breast tenders

1 cup all-purpose flour

½ teaspoon salt

¼ teaspoon freshly ground black pepper

2 eggs

1 tablespoon peanut oil, plus more for frying

1 cup crushed cornflakes

1 cup Italian-style panko bread crumbs

1 teaspoon ground paprika

For sauce: In a bowl, combine feta, buttermilk, sour cream, parsley, pepper, scallions, and garlic. Stir, then cover. Refrigerate for at least 30 minutes before serving.

For chicken: Pour buttermilk into a large, resealable plastic bag. Add chicken tenders. Seal and refrigerate for 30 minutes. Remove chicken from bag and discard buttermilk.

In a shallow bowl, combine flour, salt, and pepper.

In another shallow bowl, beat together eggs, 1 tablespoon peanut oil, and 1 tablespoon water.

In a separate shallow bowl, combine cornflakes, bread crumbs, and paprika.

Dredge tenders, one at a time, in flour, then egg mixture, then crumb mixture.

Preheat oven to 200°F and place a baking sheet inside.

Heat 1 inch peanut oil in a nonstick skillet. Fry tenders, cooking for 4 minutes per side, or until golden brown. Repeat, adding more oil, as needed, between batches. Transfer tenders to baking sheet to keep warm.

Makes 4 servings.

Honorable Mention winner in *The 2009 Old Farmer's Almanac* Reader Recipe Contest for buttermilk
Jane Estrin, Jacksonville, Florida

ROASTED RED PEPPER, MOZZARELLA, AND BASIL–STUFFED CHICKEN

TESTER'S COMMENTS

Browning the chicken (after stuffing but before baking) really kicked this recipe up a notch. I also added a little more cheese to each piece of chicken with fantastic results. This is now a regular feature at the dinner table. –S.L.P.

4 boneless, skinless chicken breast halves

1 tablespoon Italian seasoning, divided

salt and freshly ground black pepper, to taste

1 jar (12 ounces) sweet roasted red peppers, sliced into 1-inch pieces

1 bunch fresh basil leaves

8 ounces fresh mozzarella, cut into 8 slices

¼ cup freshly grated Parmesan cheese

Preheat oven to 400°F. Grease a 13x9-inch, broiler-safe casserole.

Butterfly chicken breast halves: Slice through each breast horizontally, leaving ¼-inch "hinge."

Open chicken breasts and place in casserole. Sprinkle with half of Italian seasoning and salt and pepper. On one side (half) of each breast, layer roasted red peppers, basil leaves, and 1 slice mozzarella. Fold over other side, tucking in fillings. Sprinkle with remaining Italian seasoning.

Bake for 30 to 40 minutes, or until chicken is no longer pink. Remove from oven. Turn oven to broil. Top each breast with 1 slice mozzarella. Sprinkle with Parmesan. Broil until cheese is browned and bubbly, about 5 minutes.

Makes 4 servings.

I am always looking for healthy recipes for me and my family. This is an awesome dish. Serve with roasted asparagus and a side salad.

Barbara Lepley, Meyersdale, Pennsylvania

Originally, mozzarella was made from the milk of water buffalo in Italy. More flavorful than cow's milk mozzarella, you can still get this traditional, softer variety of cheese by looking for the name "Mozzarella di bufala."

CHICKEN SPAGHETTI CASSEROLE

When you need a delicious dish for a community or potluck supper, take this along. Neighbors and friends loved it. A couple of them, unbeknownst to each other, described it as classic comfort food. When I make it again, I will add a small jar of pimentos, drained and chopped, but that's just my preference. –C.S.

3 boneless, skinless chicken breast halves

1 pound spaghetti

1 can (14.5 ounces) chicken broth

1 can (10.5 ounces) cream of chicken soup

1 can (10.5 ounces) cream of celery soup

1 can (10.5 ounces) cream of mushroom soup

1½ cups shredded cheddar cheese

Cook chicken breasts your favorite way, then chop chicken into bite-size pieces. Set aside.

Cook spaghetti according to package directions.

Preheat oven to 350°F.

In a bowl, combine chicken, spaghetti, broth, and soups. Stir to blend. Transfer to an 11x7-inch baking dish. Sprinkle with cheddar. Bake for 30 to 40 minutes, or until hot and bubbly.

Makes 5 to 6 servings.

My two sisters and I were visiting Mom and Dad in Oklahoma on a special Christmas in 2004. My mom, when I asked her, gave me a few recipes. We had such great memories, and this is the best "Chicken Spaghetti" that you will ever taste.

Mike Church, Rockford, Illinois

- Spaghetti, which means "little string" in Italian, is a thin, long, and round noodle.
- Vermicelli, meaning "little worms," can be slightly thinner or thicker than spaghetti.
- Linguine, which means "little tongues," is thin, long, flat, and a bit wider than spaghetti.

❧ CHICKEN CONTINENTAL ❧

⅓ cup all-purpose flour

salt and freshly ground black pepper or Lawry's seasoned salt, to taste

1 broiler-fryer chicken (3 pounds), cut up

4 tablespoons (½ stick) butter

1 can (10.5 ounces) cream of chicken, celery, or mushroom soup

2½ tablespoons finely minced onion

1 tablespoon finely chopped parsley

1 teaspoon salt

½ teaspoon celery flakes

⅛ teaspoon dried thyme

dash of freshly ground black pepper

1⅓ cups Minute Rice

Preheat oven to 350°F.

Combine flour and salt and pepper in a resealable plastic bag. Add chicken pieces, a few at a time, and shake to coat.

Melt butter in a skillet over medium heat. Add chicken and cook until browned on both sides. Transfer chicken to a baking sheet. Add chicken soup, onions, parsley, salt, celery flakes, thyme, pepper, and 1⅓ cups water to chicken drippings in skillet. Heat to boiling, stirring constantly.

Spread rice in a shallow 1½-quart casserole. Reserve ⅓ cup soup mixture. Pour remainder over rice and stir to moisten. Place cooked chicken on rice. Pour reserved soup mixture over chicken. Bake for 45 minutes.

Makes 4 servings.

When my daughter was born 42 years ago, my neighbor cooked a dinner for our family and this was the main course. Our whole family thought that it was delicious! It has since become a favorite for us. My daughter, now the mother of two daughters, has made it a part of her family's favorites. We even keep the tradition alive by making it for a friend who has had a baby. We tell them the recipe's tradition, and they are truly touched. Everyone has enjoyed it and asks for the recipe. It has been fun sharing this wonderful main dish! It's easy to double and make in a larger casserole.

Gloria Armstrong, Longmont, Colorado

CHICKEN AND CAJUN PORK SAUSAGE STROGANOFF

TESTER'S COMMENTS

A unique blend of cuisines, this hearty dish leaves its spiciness up to the cook. –M.S.

MAIN DISHES: POULTRY

3 tablespoons vegetable oil

3 tablespoons butter

2 boneless, skinless chicken breast halves, cut into bite-size pieces

2 links cajun pork sausage, cut into bite-size pieces

cajun seasoning, to taste

poultry seasoning, to taste

garlic powder, to taste

cayenne pepper, to taste

smoked paprika, to taste

dash of cumin

dash of chili powder

1 onion, finely chopped

2 tablespoons all-purpose flour

3 to 4 cups chicken stock

2 cans (10.5 ounces each) cream of mushroom soup

¾ cup sliced fresh mushrooms

½ cup sour cream, or to taste

freshly ground black pepper, to taste

12 ounces cooked egg noodles

Heat oil and butter in a skillet over medium heat.

Sprinkle chicken and sausage pieces with cajun and poultry seasonings, garlic powder, cayenne, paprika, cumin, and chili powder.

Transfer to skillet and brown on all sides. Add onions and cook for 2 to 3 minutes, or until translucent. Sprinkle with flour and stir, scraping bottom of skillet. Cook for 3 to 4 minutes more, stirring. Add chicken stock and bring to a boil. Reduce heat to simmer. Add mushroom soup and stir. Add mushrooms and simmer for 30 minutes. Add sour cream and stir. Season with pepper. Serve over egg noodles.

Makes 4 to 5 servings.

Spicy cajun pork sausage is one of my favorite meats to incorporate into a dish. I also love stroganoff with fresh mushrooms. I decided to use my traditional gumbo ingredients but turn it into a stroganoff. This dish is fantastic!

Sharon Schmidt, Chicago, Illinois

GRA'S BARBECUE CHICKEN

The longer these chicken legs marinate, the better their flavor will be. Overnight would be best if you have the time. –M.S.

1 tablespoon butter

½ large onion (Vidalia preferred), finely chopped

½ cup ketchup

¼ cup apple cider vinegar

4 teaspoons dark-brown sugar

1 teaspoon ground mustard

1 teaspoon sweet paprika

½ teaspoon ground white pepper

1 pound chicken legs

Melt butter in a skillet over medium heat, add onions, and cook until translucent. Add ketchup, vinegar, brown sugar, mustard, paprika, white pepper, and ¾ cup water and stir. Bring to a boil.

Pour half of sauce over chicken legs. Refrigerate to marinate for a few hours or overnight.

Preheat grill. Cook chicken legs for 20 to 25 minutes. While grilling, baste legs with remaining sauce.

Pile legs on serving dish. Drizzle with any remaining sauce. Serve with biscuits: There'll be a good puddle of sauce to sop up!

Makes 3 to 4 servings.

Gra (my grandmother) never wore a dress without an apron over it. And she never wrote down, much less read, a recipe. (She only went through third grade in school, as she was then orphaned and removed from her family tribal surroundings and made a kitchen slave in a white woman's home in a nearby town.) On a hot summer night, I would smell this sauce cooking and would run out to help Grampsy (my grandfather) to bring out a little hibachi grill. I would pile in the charcoal briquettes and sit with him until I could tell Gra that they were white-hot. Then she would bring out the chicken legs! She also would have soaked some ears of corn and put them into the coals. Then she would bring out a green bean salad and hot biscuits. The warmth of the evening and the warmth of this sweet sauce still tastes of August to me.

Doe West, Sturbridge, Massachusetts

Tongs are best for turning meat when cooking on the grill.
Piercing the flesh with a fork will let out the juices.

ROSEMARY WINE CHICKEN STEW

¼ cup extra-virgin olive oil

½ cup all-purpose flour

1 teaspoon sea salt

1 teaspoon freshly ground black pepper

1 pound boneless, skinless chicken breasts, cut into bite-size pieces

1½ tablespoons tomato paste

3 carrots, peeled and sliced

5 red potatoes, cubed

1 cup cubed rutabaga

8 ounces mushrooms, sliced

1 small onion, finely chopped

¼ cup chopped fresh parsley

2½ cups low-sodium chicken broth

2½ cups dry white wine

2 sprigs rosemary

Heat olive oil in a Dutch oven over medium heat.

In a resealable plastic bag, combine flour, salt, and pepper. Add chicken and shake to coat well.

Transfer chicken to Dutch oven and braise until crust forms. (Do not crowd chicken cubes; braise in two batches, if necessary.) Add tomato paste, carrots, potatoes, rutabaga, mushrooms, onions, and parsley. Add chicken broth, wine, and rosemary and mix well. Reduce heat, cover, and cook for 2 hours, or until vegetables are fork tender.

Makes 6 servings.

I grew up eating French foods and ate a lot of beef stews and pork stews. I wanted to create a lighter version. I used chicken and white wine instead of red wine. It's now a family favorite, much healthier for you without neglecting the traditional heartiness of this dish. It's light enough for a Sunday summer meal!

Josee Lanzi, New Port Richey, Florida

❦ Chicken Casserole ❧

Do not discount this recipe because of its simplicity; it is very easy, but also very good. It comes together quickly (I made it for supper one night after work), and you can stretch it by adding vegetables—peas, as suggested, or broccoli. The taste is similar to that of chicken divan. –L.R.

1 pound boneless, skinless chicken breasts, cooked and shredded
1 can (10.5 ounces) cream of chicken soup
1 container (16 ounces) sour cream or plain yogurt
1 sleeve Ritz crackers, crushed
½ cup (1 stick) butter or margarine, melted

Preheat oven to 350°F.

In a 13x9-inch baking dish, combine chicken, chicken soup, and sour cream. Top with crushed crackers. Pour butter over top. Bake for 30 minutes, or until golden and bubbly.

Makes 6 servings.

This was my mother's recipe, and all of my children love it. Now they are grown, and my daughter and my daughter-in-law also make it for their families. A family tradition, it's very simple, but delicious. We like it served with green peas, which my mother has actually included in the casserole sometimes.

Patricia Kiessling, Cleveland, Georgia

❦ Turkey ❧ Shepherd's Pie

The mushroom soup and turkey make this surprisingly different from traditional shepherd's pie. This is an easy and satisfying way to use leftover potatoes. –L.R.

1 pound ground turkey, cooked
¼ cup finely chopped onion
2 cups frozen mixed vegetables, thawed
1 can (10.5 ounces) cream of mushroom soup
salt and freshly ground black pepper, to taste
3 cups cooked and mashed potatoes

Preheat oven to 350°F.

In a bowl, combine turkey, onions, vegetables, mushroom soup, and salt and pepper. Pour into a 9x9-inch baking dish. Top with mashed potatoes. Bake for 1 hour, or until top is golden brown. Let sit for 5 minutes, then serve.

Makes 4 to 5 servings.

Shepherd's pie always sounded good, but I don't eat red meat, so I thought that I'd try turkey instead. It turned out great. My whole family loves it.

Pam McMunn, Davenport, Iowa

Turkey Shepherd's Pie

✿ SEA CAKES FLORENTINE ✿

Although a patty size is suggested, you can make them any manageable size; I used an ice cream scoop as a measure for appetizers (think slider-size). While a traditional Florentine treatment would use the garlic spinach as a bed, here it serves well as a topping. If time allows, make your own béarnaise sauce (opposite page). Tasters gave these cakes four stars—and I'll give them one more for a full five stars. –C.S.

Cakes:

2 sleeves Ritz crackers, divided

1 can (16 ounces) lump crabmeat, with liquid

1 egg, beaten

10 raw shrimp, peeled, deveined, and chopped

5 or 6 small (bay) scallops, chopped (optional)

½ onion, chopped

½ bell pepper, any color, chopped

1 tablespoon chopped fresh parsley

1 teaspoon Old Bay seasoning

salt and freshly ground black pepper, to taste

vegetable oil

Garlic Spinach:

2 tablespoons (¼ stick) butter

2 cloves garlic, minced

1 to 2 bags fresh baby spinach (6 ounces per serving)

1 package béarnaise sauce mix (makes 1¼ cups)

For cakes: Crush 1½ sleeves of crackers and put into a bowl. Add crabmeat with liquid, egg, shrimp, scallops (if using), onions, bell peppers, parsley, Old Bay, and salt and pepper. Mix well.

Cover bottom of a frying pan with oil.

Finely crush remaining crackers and transfer to a plate.

Make patties of seafood mixture. Press into crushed crackers to coat both sides. Fry for 20 minutes, or until golden brown, turning once.

For garlic spinach: In a frying pan over medium heat, melt butter. Add garlic and cook until softened. Add spinach and stir until wilted. Do not overcook. Set aside.

Prepare béarnaise sauce according to package directions or make your own (see opposite page). Keep cakes warm in oven, if necessary.

Serve sea cakes topped with garlic spinach and béarnaise sauce.

Makes 4 to 6 servings.

Crab cakes appealed to me, but I never found what I'd imagined them to be, anywhere. I experimented, as usual, and made my own. I knew when I had what I was looking for and make these for my family regularly. It's a favorite. This is a fast, simple, delicious, gourmet- and restaurant-quality meal. I cook for the elderly and use this recipe often, as it is easy for them to eat.

JoAnn Ashfaq, South Yarmouth, Massachusetts

MAIN DISHES: SEAFOOD

BÉARNAISE SAUCE

¼ cup white-wine vinegar
¼ cup white wine
1 shallot, minced
3 tablespoons chopped fresh tarragon, divided
salt and freshly ground black pepper, to taste
3 egg yolks
1 cup (2 sticks) butter, melted

In a saucepan, combine vinegar, wine, shallots, 1 tablespoon tarragon, and salt and pepper. Bring to a boil, then simmer for 5 to 7 minutes, or until reduced to 3 to 4 tablespoons. Set aside to cool slightly.

Place egg yolks and vinegar mixture in a blender or food processor. Process for 20 to 30 seconds. Add butter in a stream while processing. Add remaining tarragon and process in quick bursts. Thin, if desired, with a spoonful of white wine. Serve immediately.

Almanac favorite

Béarnaise sauce is made from butter, egg yolks, and white-wine vinegar
and flavored with shallots and herbs. It is considered to be a "child"
of hollandaise sauce, one of the five mother sauces in French cuisine
(others: béchamel, espagnole, tomate, velouté).

CLAMS À LA DENISE

TESTER'S COMMENTS

Yummy! With asparagus, this dish made for a "spa" lunch. It's a great recipe to keep on hand. If you do your own clamming, you'll know that rinsing as described is very important. –C.S.

3 dozen fresh cherrystone or littleneck clams

3 tablespoons butter

1 tablespoon olive oil

1 onion, minced

1 large clove garlic, minced

½ teaspoon dried oregano

¼ to ½ teaspoon crushed red pepper flakes,
   or to taste

salt, to taste

⅓ cup chopped fresh parsley

¼ cup dry white wine

Scrub clams well under running cold water to remove sand and seaweed.

In a pot, bring 1 cup water to a boil. Add clams and return to boiling. Reduce heat to medium-low, cover, and cook for 6 to 8 minutes, or until shells open. Discard any that do not open. Transfer clams to a pot or bowl. Let broth stand until sand settles.

In a saucepan over medium heat, melt butter with olive oil. Add onions, garlic, oregano, red pepper flakes, and salt. Cook until onions are tender, stirring occasionally. Add parsley and wine, and cook for 2 minutes.

Discard top half-shell from each clam. Put clams in bottom shell on a serving plate.

Carefully, without disturbing sand on bottom of pot, ladle clam broth into onion mixture. Heat until hot. Pour over clams.

Makes 10 to 12 servings.

I wanted a good recipe for clams that could be either an appetizer or a dinner. With some fiddling around, I came up with this dinner version. Serve with good Italian bread or chop clams, add to onion mixture, and serve over pasta.

Denise Seitter, Ridgefield Park, New Jersey

Clams, mussels, and oysters should be wrapped in wet towels or a
wet paper bag and kept refrigerated. Stored this way, they can keep for 2 to 3 days.

MAIN DISHES: SEAFOOD

❧ CLAMBAKE POTATOES ❧

6 russet baking potatoes

2 cups sour cream

1 can (8 ounces) minced clams, drained, liquid reserved

¼ cup finely minced fresh chives or 2 tablespoons freeze-dried chopped chives

1 teaspoon salt

1 to 2 teaspoons freshly ground black pepper, or to taste

¼ to ⅓ cup clam juice or broth

Preheat oven to 375°F.

Scrub potatoes, then prick bottoms several times with a fork. Bake on oven rack or baking sheet for 50 minutes, or until tender. Cool completely.

Reduce oven to 350°F.

Cut potatoes in half lengthwise. Scoop flesh from each piece, keeping skins intact.

In a bowl, mash flesh with sour cream, adding up to ⅓ cup clam liquid to make a soft mash. Mix in clams, chives, salt, and pepper. Add enough clam juice to achieve desired consistency. Stuff generously into potato shells and place on baking sheet. Bake for 20 to 25 minutes, or until hot and top of filling is browned.

Makes 12 stuffed potato halves.

I was an ovo-lacto-pesco vegetarian for over 15 years and needed simple recipes that I could make that would be appealing to my nonvegetarian family. This was something we all enjoyed. It makes a nice supper served with a big green salad full of romaine, escarole, tomatoes, avocados, and cucumbers and a side dish of baked carrots with honey glaze.

Samantha Gray, Glen Cove, New York

Ancient Chinese herbalists suggested eating chives as an antidote to poison.

❧ MY MAINE CRAB CAKES ❧

TESTER'S COMMENTS

Use the best-quality crab that you can afford. Cream cheese makes these cakes a bit richer than most, and the heat of the cayenne perks them up. –C.S.

1 pound crabmeat, picked over
¼ cup diced onion
¼ cup diced red bell pepper
3 cups bread crumbs, divided
½ cup mayonnaise
2 ounces cream cheese, softened
1 tablespoon Dijon-style mustard
1 egg, slightly beaten
½ teaspoon dried tarragon
⅛ teaspoon cayenne pepper
⅛ teaspoon salt
2 tablespoons vegetable oil
lemon wedges, for garnish

In a bowl, combine crabmeat, onions, bell peppers, and ½ cup bread crumbs.

In another bowl, beat together mayonnaise, cream cheese, mustard, egg, tarragon, cayenne, and salt. Fold mayonnaise mixture into crabmeat mixture. Cover and refrigerate for 30 minutes. (Mixture should be moist and loose; if it is not, add more mayonnaise.)

Place remaining bread crumbs in a shallow bowl. Using an oval soup spoon (or the like), drop spoonfuls of mixture onto crumbs and form into patties, coating each side with crumbs.

Heat oil in skillet. Carefully add crab cakes and cook until golden brown, turning once. Serve with lemon wedges

Makes about 12 servings.

My love for going crabbing led me to make this recipe. I love crab cakes and could never find a recipe that I liked. After many sad attempts, I finally came up with this.

Debra Bartnick, Frankfort, Maine

Years ago, any product called "Dijon mustard" had
to come from the Dijon region of France.

✒ BEST-EVER HAWAIIAN SHRIMP TACOS ✒

The recipe requires a little planning, especially if you infuse your own vinegar. (A mango-flavor rice vinegar is available in some stores, but not everywhere.) If you have neither the time to infuse vinegar nor a place to buy it, peel and dice a ripe mango and combine it with the pineapple and ½ cup rice vinegar. Another quick option is to use fresh-cut, packaged pineapple. One type of bean—pinto or black—is a fine substitute for blended beans, which are also hard to find. Once done, this combination is filling and delicious. One taster gave the dish two thumbs up. Another taster said that she could eat the salsa with anything. I put the pineapple salsa atop a tuna steak for dinner and felt like I was on a tropical vacation. –M.A.J.

Pineapple salsa:

1 can (15.5 ounces) blended beans or an equivalent combination of black, pinto, and great northern beans, drained

1 pineapple, chopped into small chunks

½ bunch fresh cilantro, chopped

chipotle seasoning, to taste

½ cup mango-infused rice vinegar (see Tester's Comments)

Shrimp:

1 pound raw shrimp, peeled and deveined, or chicken tenders, or your favorite fish cut into chunks

2 tablespoons olive oil

1 tablespoon McCormick's Smokehouse Maple seasoning

2 teaspoons garlic powder

2 teaspoons onion salt

½ teaspoon chipotle seasoning, or to taste

Wasabi dressing:

½ cup ranch dressing

½ tablespoon wasabi sauce, or to taste

12 corn tortillas or tacos

For pineapple salsa: In a bowl, combine beans, pineapple, and cilantro. Sprinkle with chipotle seasoning and add vinegar. Mix and set aside.

For shrimp: In a bowl, toss shrimp in oil to coat. Sprinkle with maple seasoning, garlic powder, onion salt, and chipotle seasoning. Toss again. In a skillet over medium heat, cook for 5 to 6 minutes, or until pink.

For wasabi dressing: In a bowl, combine ranch dressing and wasabi sauce.

To assemble: Warm tortillas according to package directions. Dribble wasabi dressing on each, add shrimp, and top with salsa.

Makes 4 servings.

It all started with the pineapple salsa. I originally made it for salmon steaks on rice, and it evolved to many uses. I have to make these once a week now.

Leslie Shepard, Pagosa Springs, Colorado

Baked "Manicotti" Crepes à la Mama

Instead of traditional manicotti shells, this recipe uses crepes. The crepe batter has the consistency of cream and cooks up easily and quickly in a skillet, if a griddle is not available. The result is tender, light, and yummy. These are perfect as appetizers or a main dish. Enjoy! –C.S.

Crepes:

5 eggs

1¼ cups all-purpose flour

¼ teaspoon salt

olive oil, for griddle

Filling:

1 tablespoon butter or margarine

¼ cup finely chopped onion

1 pound ground beef

1 egg, beaten

1 package (10 ounces) frozen chopped spinach, thawed and drained

1 tablespoon grated Parmesan cheese, plus more for sprinkling

1 tablespoon finely chopped fresh parsley

1 teaspoon salt

¼ teaspoon freshly ground black pepper

4 cups marinara sauce, divided

For crepes: Preheat griddle.

In a bowl, combine eggs, flour, salt, and 1¼ cups water. Beat until smooth. Allow batter to sit for about 20 minutes.

Brush griddle lightly with olive oil. Spoon 2 tablespoons batter onto griddle and spread it quickly with back of spoon, making a 6x4-inch oval crepe. Cook for 20 to 30 seconds, or until top surface is dry but bottom is not brown. Carefully flip over and cook for 20 seconds more. Set aside to cool. Repeat with remaining batter. Stack crepes one on top of another until ready to fill.

For filling: Melt butter in a skillet over medium heat, add onions, and cook until golden brown. Add beef and cook until thoroughly browned. Add egg, spinach, Parmesan, parsley, salt, and pepper. Mix well.

To assemble: Preheat oven to 350°F. Coat bottoms of two 13x9-inch baking dishes with 1 cup marinara sauce each.

Place 1 heaping tablespoon filling on crepe, then roll it up. Closely pack rolled crepes in one layer in prepared pans. Coat with remaining sauce and sprinkle with Parmesan. Cover with aluminum foil. Bake for 30 minutes.

Makes 12 servings.

My Italian mother usually served this dish on holidays. Although we had American-style turkey, ham, or roast beef on Thanksgiving, Christmas, and Easter, we also had Mama's baked "manicotti" on the side! I now make it for my children and grandchildren.
Rose Scalise, Prospect Heights, Illinois

❧ HOMEMADE MAC AND CHEEZ ❧

On reading this through the first time, I thought the measurements were off. After making it and then tasting it, I realized that the measurements for flour, milk, and cheese that I have been using for years were off! Very smooth and creamy mac and cheese right here! We loved it. I crisp-cooked and crumbled bacon to mix in before baking (I usually add ham). It is delicious! –M.S.

1½ cups elbow macaroni

4 tablespoons (½ stick) butter

½ teaspoon salt

½ teaspoon freshly ground black pepper

¼ cup all-purpose flour

1¾ cups milk

1 cup shredded cheese

Preheat oven to 350°F. Grease a 13x9-inch baking dish.

Cook macaroni according to package directions.

Melt butter in a skillet. Add salt and pepper and stir. Add flour and cook over low heat, stirring constantly. Add milk and whisk to combine. Add cheese and stir until it melts.

Drain macaroni and pour into prepared dish. Pour cheese mixture over macaroni and stir to coat. Bake for 30 minutes, or until golden brown.

Makes 4 servings.

My grandma always made this when we had get-togethers and family reunions, and I just love it. I make it for all of our family gatherings.

Kari Gilkison, Marion, Indiana

The best way to reheat leftover macaroni
and cheese is on the stove. Add a small amount of milk to the
leftovers and warm over low heat, stirring often.

GRACE COSTA'S SOUTH INDIAN–STYLE MAC AND CHEESE

TESTER'S COMMENTS

Do not fear the garlic or spices required in this recipe. The result is a rich, flavorful, creamy mac and cheese, with a hint of mystery that most people will enjoy. Guests will wonder, What is in this dish that makes it taste so good? –C.S.

Topping:
½ cup fresh bread crumbs
¼ cup grated Asiago cheese
½ teaspoon paprika
8 ounces elbow macaroni

Sauce:
½ teaspoon garam masala
½ teaspoon salt
¼ teaspoon freshly ground black pepper
¼ teaspoon ground turmeric
¼ teaspoon ground cayenne pepper

3 tablespoons unsalted butter
1½ teaspoons ginger garlic paste (see opposite page)
3 tablespoons all-purpose flour
3 cups milk (not skim)
2 cups shredded sharp cheddar cheese

Preheat oven to 350°F. Generously grease a 2-quart casserole.

For topping: In a bowl, combine bread crumbs, Asiago, and paprika. Set aside.

Cook macaroni al dente, according to package directions. Drain and put into prepared casserole.

For sauce: In another bowl, combine garam masala, salt, pepper, turmeric, and cayenne. Set aside.

Melt butter in a saucepan over medium heat. Add ginger garlic paste as butter is melting. (If added to hot butter, paste will spatter wildly; heat slowly in melting butter.) Add spice mixture and cook for 2 to 3 minutes, stirring constantly. Add flour and cook for 1 to 2 minutes over medium heat. Add milk slowly, stirring constantly until mixture boils for at least 1 minute, or until incorporated. Remove from heat and fold in shredded cheese.

To assemble: Pour sauce over cooked macaroni and stir gently to combine. Sprinkle with bread crumb mixture. Bake for 25 to 30 minutes, or until bubbly.

Makes 6 to 8 servings.

This recipe came from Grace Costa, my late mother-in-law. She was raised in Kerala in South India, commonly referred to as "the spice coast of India," one of nine children of a Syrian Christian minister. Entertaining parishioners over meals was a way of life growing up. She became an incredibly accomplished woman, the first trained industrial nurse in all of India, but she always loved to cook. No family gathering, church event, or community event would be complete without a contribution from her kitchen. She cooked by taste and could salvage even the most terrifying culinary disaster with a few quick instructions.

John Pierce, Dublin, New Hampshire

GINGER GARLIC PASTE
Ginger garlic paste provides the background flavor of many South Indian dishes. It can be purchased at Indian grocery stores or made at home by using one-third fresh garlic to two-thirds fresh ginger by weight. Process in a food processor, using as little water as necessary to make a paste. Refrigerated, it will keep for at least a week.

BETTER-THAN-MOTHER-IN-LAW'S CREAMY MAC AND CHEESE

With three kinds of cheese, this is really good creamy mac and cheese. In fact, it's excellent. –C.S.

2 tablespoons (¼ stick) butter, divided

1 teaspoon salt

1 box (16 ounces) elbow macaroni

3 cups milk

½ cup cubed Velveeta

1 can (10.5 ounces) Campbell's cheese soup

1 cup shredded Colby cheese

2 cups shredded cheddar cheese, divided

Preheat oven to 350°F. Grease a 13x9-inch casserole or baking dish with 1 tablespoon butter.

In a stockpot, bring 8 cups water to a boil. Add salt and macaroni. Cook macaroni al dente, according to package directions, drain, and return to pot.

In a saucepan over medium heat, combine milk, remaining butter, Velveeta, and cheese soup. Cook for 10 to 15 minutes, or until cheese is melted, stirring often.

Pour cheese sauce over macaroni. Add Colby and 1 cup cheddar. Stir to combine. Transfer to prepared casserole. Top with remaining cheese. Bake for 20 minutes.

Makes 8 servings.

My beautiful, perfect mother-in-law makes a great mac and cheese with flour. Every time I followed her recipe, it came out dry. With two skinny kids in braces who found it easy to eat mac and cheese, and not wanting to feed them from a box every night, I combined parts of my mother-in-law's recipe with the creamy texture that the kids liked from the boxes. This recipe stays creamy, never dry, even after reheating it in the microwave. Now, my mother-in-law asks me to make the mac and cheese!

Elizabeth Browning, Lebanon, Ohio

U.S. president Thomas Jefferson is thought to have
popularized macaroni (sometimes topped with cheese) by serving
it to his guests during his time at the White House.

MAIN DISHES: PASTA & RICE

SPAGHETTI WITH ASPARAGUS AND BACON

Yummy! The cheese sauce coats the spaghetti and crispy asparagus nicely, and the crumbled bacon adds crunch and saltiness. –M.A.J.

8 ounces spaghetti

1 pound asparagus, trimmed and cut into 1- to 2-inch pieces

4 tablespoons olive oil, divided

4 tablespoons (½ stick) butter

2 cloves garlic, minced

¼ cup grated Parmesan cheese, plus more for serving

6 ounces bacon, cooked and crumbled

Preheat oven to 400°F.

Cook spaghetti al dente, according to package directions. Drain, reserving ¼ cup cooking water.

Toss asparagus with 1 tablespoon olive oil. Place on a baking sheet and roast for 8 minutes, turning once halfway through cooking time.

Melt butter in a skillet over medium heat with remaining olive oil. Add garlic and sauté for 30 seconds, or until fragrant. Add pasta water and Parmesan, followed by spaghetti and asparagus. Stir gently and cook over low heat for 1 minute. Add bacon and toss to combine. Transfer to a bowl or platter. Serve with extra Parmesan and crusty bread, if desired.

Makes 4 servings.

I wanted to do a take on spaghetti carbonara that didn't involve the egg. This turned out deliciously. Great as a main dish with some lean protein added as well. It's a family favorite!

Robin Williams, Huntersville, North Carolina

To keep asparagus spears fresh for a day or two
after purchasing, place them upright in a jar and add an inch
of cold water. Store the jar in the refrigerator.

Kat's Tortellini Salad

We loved this salad! It's simple to prepare, and the flavors mixed well. It's great to have on hand in warm weather. –M.S.

1 package (9 ounces) tortellini

1 package (10 ounces) fresh spinach, torn into bite-size pieces (optional)

1 jar (6 ounces) marinated artichoke hearts, drained and sliced

1½ cups diced mozzarella cheese

1 cup sliced ripe olives

⅓ cup chopped sweet roasted red peppers

1 cup red-wine salad dressing

¼ cup grated Parmesan cheese

Cook tortellini according to package directions. Drain, then chill.

In a bowl, combine pasta, spinach (if using), artichoke hearts, mozzarella, olives, and roasted peppers. Add salad dressing and toss to coat. Sprinkle with Parmesan.

Makes 4 to 6 servings.

This is a quick and easy dish that my better half made for me. Now I make it for her when I want to "cook dinner."
Jim Bodie, West Henrietta, New York

Fresh off the tree, both green and black olives are
extremely bitter, so they have to be cured before they are eaten.

CREAMY SPAGHETTI TORTE WITH BACON

TESTER'S COMMENTS

For such a fancy-looking dish, this was easy to prepare. Tasters loved the added texture of mushrooms and bacon in every mouthful. —S.L.P.

MAIN DISHES: PASTA & RICE

1 pound bacon, coarsely chopped

8 ounces sliced fresh mushrooms

salt and coarsely ground black pepper, to taste

1 cup heavy cream

2 cups grated Parmesan cheese

12 ounces spaghetti, cooked al dente and drained

⅓ cup chopped fresh parsley

2 eggs, beaten

Preheat oven to 375°F. Butter a 9-inch springform pan.

In a skillet over medium-high heat, cook bacon until crispy. Remove bacon to paper towels to drain.

Add mushrooms to skillet with bacon drippings and cook for 4 minutes, or until tender. Season with salt and pepper. Whisk in heavy cream, then add Parmesan. Reduce heat to medium-low and cook, stirring, until cheese melts. Remove from heat. Add spaghetti and toss to coat evenly. Add bacon and parsley, then stir in eggs until well blended.

Press spaghetti mixture into prepared pan. Bake for 40 minutes, or until set. Let stand 5 minutes. Remove sides of pan and cut into cakelike slices.

Makes 6 to 8 servings.

Third-prize winner in *The 2012 Old Farmer's Almanac* Reader Recipe Contest for bacon
Karen Kuebler, Dallas, Texas

If pasta sticks together after draining, plunge it quickly
back into boiling water to which you have added a tablespoon
of olive oil. Drain; your pasta should come unstuck.

ꙮ SPINACH RONI CASSEROLE ꙮ

After the first bite, one friend trying this dish immediately requested the recipe. Another said that it was her favorite recipe of several that she had taste-tested for me. Everybody at the table took seconds and (small) thirds. Yum! –D.T.

1 box (6.4 ounces) Creamy Four-Cheese Rice-A-Roni

1 can (13.5 ounces) spinach, drained, or equivalent amount frozen, thawed, and drained

2 eggs, beaten

2 cups shredded cheddar cheese

1 cup milk

½ cup melted butter, plus more for Rice-A-Roni

1 teaspoon salt

Preheat oven to 325°F. Grease a shallow, 2-quart casserole.

Prepare Rice-A-Roni according to package directions.

In a bowl, combine Rice-A-Roni, spinach, eggs, cheddar, milk, butter, and salt. Mix well.

Pour into prepared casserole. Bake for 1 hour, or until top is golden.

Makes 6 to 8 servings.

When my two sons were young, we'd be shopping in the grocery store and they would get attention by begging me to buy some spinach and laughing about it! Now they are both grown and married, and it is a must that I prepare this dish for every holiday and family gathering. It's our undying family tradition.

Virginia Curtis, Gadsden, Alabama

To test an egg for freshness, put it into a
bowl of cold water. If it sinks to the bottom, then it
is suitable for use. If it floats, it is too old.

APPLE CIDER RISOTTO WITH CARROT CONFETTI

If multicolor carrots are available to you, use them. The "ohs" and "ahs" from tasters came from both the pleasing look of the dish and the taste. A great way to dress up risotto. –S.L.P.

2 cups chopped carrots in variety of colors (e.g., orange, yellow, purple), plus some rounds, or "coins," for garnish

1½ teaspoons olive oil

1 cup apple cider

1 apple, peeled, cored, and cut into ½-inch pieces

½ cup dry white wine

5 cups vegetable stock

1½ tablespoons butter

½ cup minced shallots

2 cups Arborio rice

2 tablespoons minced fresh sage leaves, plus whole leaves, for garnish

¾ cup shredded Asiago cheese

salt and freshly ground black pepper, to taste

Preheat oven to 350°F.

Spread carrots on a baking sheet in a single layer. Drizzle with olive oil and toss to coat. Roast for 10 to 15 minutes, or until lightly browned, not crisp. Set aside, reserving coins separately.

Heat apple cider to boiling. Pour over apple pieces. Set aside for 3 minutes. Strain apple pieces and reserve cider. Add wine to reserved cider. Combine apple pieces with chopped carrots.

Heat stock to boiling. Reduce heat to low.

Melt butter in a soup pot. Add shallots and cook until translucent. Add rice and stir to coat. Add cider–wine mixture and cook, stirring frequently, until all liquid is absorbed. Add warm stock, 1 cup at a time, stirring constantly. When rice has absorbed most of liquid, repeat, using remaining stock. Add sage, carrot–apple mixture, Asiago, and salt and pepper. Stir until cheese melts. Transfer to a serving bowl. Garnish with carrot coins and sage leaves.

Makes 6 to 8 servings.

Second-prize winner in *The 2014 Old Farmer's Almanac* Reader Recipe Contest for carrots
Mona Grandbois, Biddeford, Maine

Arborio rice is high in starch, which is
what gives risotto its classic creamy texture.

MAIN DISHES: PASTA & RICE

BREADS

TWICE-PEPPERED BACON AND BUTTERMILK SCONES

TESTER'S COMMENTS

Love these peppery scones! They are perfect with anything, from eggs to soup. The contributor's comments say it all. Or almost all: Tasters sang their praises. –C.S.

1 cup buttermilk

1 egg

3 cups all-purpose flour

1 tablespoon baking powder

2 teaspoons freshly ground black pepper

1 teaspoon salt

¼ teaspoon cayenne pepper

8 tablespoons (1 stick) unsalted butter, chilled and cut into small pieces

1½ cups grated Gruyère cheese

½ cup crisp cooked bacon, finely crumbled

Preheat oven to 425°F. Line a baking sheet with parchment paper.

In a bowl, whisk buttermilk and egg until well blended. Set aside 2 tablespoons for glaze.

Put flour, baking powder, black pepper, salt, and cayenne into a food processor. Pulse for 1 second four times, or until combined. Scatter cold butter pieces evenly over dry ingredients and pulse for 1 second 12 to 14 times, or until mixture resembles coarse crumbs. Transfer to a bowl. Add Gruyère and bacon. With a sturdy rubber spatula, fold in buttermilk–egg mixture (except that reserved for glaze) until large clumps form. Mix dough until it just comes together. For tender scones, handle as little as possible and work quickly.

Turn out onto a lightly floured work surface and gently pat into a ball. Flatten into a circle about 8 inches wide and ¾ of an inch thick. Cut into 8 wedges.

Place wedges on prepared baking sheet, about 2 inches apart. Brush lightly with reserved buttermilk–egg glaze. Bake for 12 to 15 minutes, or until golden brown. Serve warm.

Makes 8 scones.

The Gruyère cheese, black and cayenne peppers, and salty bacon blend magically to flavor these tender and buttery scones. They're so simple to put together. They are the perfect beginning for a special breakfast or brunch (they're a Christmas morning tradition in our home) and are also excellent as a hearty accompaniment to soups or salads.

Janice Elder, Charlotte, North Carolina

BREADS: SAVORY

❦ MATTIE'S BISCUITS ❧

TESTER'S COMMENTS

Good biscuit recipes are hard to come by, but these biscuits are great. They were not as heavy as I anticipated them to be. Bacon grease: Who would have thought? I can't help thinking of making biscuits now every time I cook bacon! –M.S.

---

2 cups all-purpose flour
1 tablespoon baking powder
½ teaspoon salt
½ cup bacon drippings or shortening
⅔ cup milk (more or less)

Preheat oven to 400°F.

In a bowl, sift flour with baking powder and salt. Cut in bacon drippings until mixture resembles coarse crumbs. Stir in milk until dough is soft and moist and pulls away from sides of bowl. Turn out onto a lightly floured work surface.

Sift a little flour over dough, then pat out with floured fingers to about a ½-inch thickness. Cut out circles with 2- or 3-inch biscuit cutter, depending on desired size.

Place on ungreased baking sheet: together for soft sides, 1 inch apart for crisp sides. Bake for 12 to 15 minutes, or until browned.

Makes 10 three-inch or 16 two-inch biscuits.

My mother-in-law, Mattie, taught me to make these biscuits before I married her son. On the advice of my own mother, I asked his mother to share her recipe. Of course, her version was "a fistful of this and a pinch of that," but I figured out the measurements and continued her tradition. By the time our children had begun spending time at their grandmother's, she had switched to the "whop, whop" canned refrigerator biscuits.

One Saturday morning, I served my homemade biscuits for breakfast. My son James—about 6 at the time—commented, "Why aren't your biscuits like Granny's?"

"Because mine are made from scratch," I bragged.

"From SCRAPS?????!!! No wonder Granny's are better!"

However, when James grew up, he invited his fiancée to our house to learn to make "Mattie's biscuits."

Evelyn Brown, Fayetteville, Arkansas

❧ SPICED CARROT BISCUITS WITH SALTED CARAMEL BUTTER ❧

Cooking and puréeing the carrots takes some time. If you want, prepare them the day before. Refrigerate the carrots until ready to use. These biscuits—so flavorful and rich with butter—are scrumptious alone. The caramel butter is like icing on a cake. –H.S.

Biscuits:

3½ cups all-purpose flour

½ cup packed brown sugar

1 tablespoon plus 2 teaspoons baking powder

1 teaspoon pumpkin pie spice

½ teaspoon salt

1 cup (2 sticks) cold butter, cut into pieces

1½ cups puréed cooked carrots (about 2 pounds fresh)

⅔ cup plus 1 tablespoon buttermilk, divided

⅓ cup golden raisins

Salted caramel butter:

½ cup (1 stick) butter, softened

¼ cup thick caramel sauce, store-bought or homemade (see below)

pinch of salt

For biscuits: Preheat oven to 425°F. Lightly grease a baking sheet.

In a bowl, stir together flour, brown sugar, baking powder, pumpkin pie spice, and salt. Cut in butter until mixture resembles coarse crumbs. Add carrots and ⅔ cup buttermilk and stir just until combined.

Turn out dough onto a lightly floured work surface. Sprinkle dough with raisins. Knead 10 times. Roll dough to about a 1-inch thickness. Cut out circles with a 2½-inch biscuit cutter. Gather and reroll dough as necessary to use all of it.

Place biscuits 1 inch apart on prepared baking sheet. Bake for 20 minutes, or until golden brown. Brush tops with remaining 1 tablespoon buttermilk.

For salted caramel butter: In a bowl, beat together butter, caramel sauce, and salt until combined. Serve with biscuits.

Makes 12 biscuits.

Third-prize winner in *The 2015 Old Farmer's Almanac* Reader Recipe Contest for carrots
Crystal Schlueter, Northglenn, Colorado

CARAMEL SAUCE

Combine 1 cup packed brown sugar, 1 cup heavy cream, and ¼ cup (½ stick) unsalted butter in a heavy saucepan. Boil for 8 minutes, stirring often. Pour into a heatproof bowl. The sauce will thicken as it cools. Makes about 2½ cups.

❦ BUTTERMILK HOT ROLLS ❧

These rolls were delicious! I make a lot of bread, especially Finnish bread, and the honey in this recipe is the secret! That, and the buttermilk. This is the recipe I will be using from now on. –M.S.

1 cup lukewarm (105° to 115°F) buttermilk
1 package (2¼ teaspoons) active dry yeast
1 tablespoon plus ¼ cup sugar or honey, divided
⅓ cup butter, melted and cooled
1 teaspoon salt
2½ cups all-purpose flour, divided
½ teaspoon baking soda

Preheat oven to 350°F. Grease a large bowl.

In a bowl, mix together buttermilk, yeast, and 1 tablespoon sugar. Set aside for 5 minutes. Add butter, ¼ cup sugar, and salt and stir.

In another bowl, combine ½ cup flour and baking soda. Add to yeast mixture. Gradually add more flour, beating thoroughly for 5 minutes and adding only enough flour to make dough firm enough to handle.

Turn dough into prepared bowl. Cover and set aside for 30 minutes to 1 hour to rise.

Punch down dough. Shape into balls and place on a baking sheet. Cover and set aside to double in bulk. Bake for 20 minutes, or until golden brown.

Makes 18 rolls.

I came up with this recipe when we had our own milk and cream. I made butter and needed ways to use the buttermilk. There are always biscuits and muffins and pancakes that my family of seven sons and one husband loved, but they still ask for these rolls at our special get-togethers—only now I buy the buttermilk!

Paula S. Olney, Millersburg, Ohio

❧ AVOCADO BREAD ❧

Spread with a blend of softened cream cheese, lemon juice, and grated lemon zest, this loaf is divine. It goes nicely with fruit salad, and because I made it in March, I discovered it to be a suitably colored option for a St. Patrick's Day treat. –C.S.

2 cups all-purpose flour

¾ cup sugar

1½ teaspoons baking powder

½ teaspoon baking soda

½ teaspoon salt

1 egg

½ cup mashed avocado (1 medium avocado)

½ cup buttermilk

½ cup chopped pecans

Preheat oven to 375°F. Grease a 9x5-inch loaf pan.

In a bowl, combine flour, sugar, baking powder, baking soda, and salt. Whisk to blend thoroughly.

In another bowl, beat together egg and avocado. Stir in buttermilk. Add to dry ingredients and blend well. Stir in pecans.

Pour into the prepared pan and bake for 50 to 60 minutes, or until a toothpick inserted into the center comes out clean.

Makes 1 loaf.

Almanac favorite

Substitute mashed avocado for butter in baked goods. You will add vitamins and minerals as well as reduce calories and fat.

❧ FALL HARVEST SQUASH ROLLS ❧

4 tablespoons active dry yeast
1 cup lukewarm (105° to 115°F) water
1⅓ cups vegetable shortening
1 cup sugar
4 eggs
2 cups cooked and mashed winter squash
2 cups warm milk
8 cups all-purpose flour, plus more as needed
2 teaspoons salt

Dissolve yeast in warm water. Set aside until foamy.

In a bowl, cream shortening with sugar. Beat in eggs. Add squash and mix until blended. Add warm milk and yeast mixture. Slowly add flour and salt. Continue to mix until dough pulls away from side of bowl. Add flour as needed to make a soft dough, being careful not to add too much. Let dough rise, covered, until doubled in size. Punch down, cover, then let rise again until doubled.

Preheat oven to 375°F. Grease two 9-inch cake pans.

Divide dough into four equal pieces, then divide each quarter into 12 pieces. Shape each piece into a ball.

Place balls in single layer, touching, in prepared pans. Cover and let rise until doubled. Bake for 20 minutes, or until lightly browned. Remove from pans and set aside to cool.

Makes 4 dozen rolls.

These rolls have been served at Kimball family Thanksgiving dinners as far back as anyone can remember.
Donna Kimball, Beech Hill Farm, Hopkinton, New Hampshire

Not all yeasts are the same. Active dry yeast needs to be dissolved in liquid before using.
Instant yeast can be mixed right into dry ingredients.

BREADS: SAVORY

SWEET POTICA (SWEET BREAD)

TESTER'S COMMENTS

Even if you have never made yeast bread, you can master this—and you will be glad that you did. It melts in your mouth; not a crumb remained of our test loaf. The secret is to roll the dough to be extremely thin. And consider this: 1 pound each of walnuts and brown sugar was more filling than I could use; ¾ of a pound of each would be plenty. Also, if you like, mix 1 tablespoon cinnamon with the brown sugar before sprinkling and add 1 cup raisins with the nuts. The batter made one very large loaf that spread horizontally on the pan while baking. To get a loaf shape, divide the dough into two balls after the first rise and then proceed as directed, rolling and filling it, making two loaves. The smaller portions will fit into loaf pans. This way, too, you'll have one loaf to serve and one for another day! –M.A.J.

Dough:

1 package (2¼ teaspoons) active dry yeast

½ cup lukewarm (105° to 115°F) water

¼ cup plus 1 teaspoon sugar, divided

½ cup scalded milk

¼ cup (½ stick) melted butter

1 teaspoon salt

1 egg, lightly beaten

3½ to 4 cups all-purpose flour, divided

Filling:

½ cup (1 stick) plus 3 tablespoons melted butter, divided

1 pound finely ground walnuts

1 pound brown sugar

For dough: Dissolve yeast in water with 1 teaspoon sugar. Set aside until foamy.

In a bowl, combine milk, ¼ cup sugar, butter, salt, egg, and 2 cups flour. Add yeast mixture and stir.

Mix in enough of remaining flour until dough is not sticking to fingers. Turn out onto a lightly floured work surface and knead for 5 to 10 minutes.

Place in a well-greased bowl, cover, and let rise until doubled.

Once dough has risen, punch down. Roll into a very thin rectangle.

For filling: Cover dough with ½ cup melted butter. Sprinkle with walnuts and brown sugar. Roll dough lengthwise like a snake. Pinch ends. Place rolled dough seam side down in well-greased 13x9-inch pan, cover, and let rise until nearly doubled.

Preheat oven to 350°F.

Bake for 1 hour. Remove from oven and baste with remaining 3 tablespoons melted butter.

Makes 18 to 24 servings, depending on thickness of slices.

This recipe came from my paternal grandmother, who was born in Croatia.

Joyce Adkins, Perkasie, Pennsylvania

BREADS: SWEET

KILLER BREAD

This bread has a lovely crust due, I suspect, to the Dutch oven. And it has wonderful flavor and density. The Dutch oven technique may need to be mastered, as it fit only if placed on the lowest oven rack. This proved to be too close to the heat element; the bottom crust got a bit dark. If desired, this recipe can be halved easily. –D.T.

1 cup lukewarm (105° to 115°F)
  water
1 teaspoon honey
2½ teaspoons active dry yeast
5 cups all-purpose flour
¼ cup sugar
1 teaspoon salt
⅓ cup powdered milk
2 tablespoons vegetable oil

In a bowl, combine water and honey. Sprinkle yeast on top and set aside for 5 minutes, or until foamy.

In another bowl, mix together flour, sugar, and salt. Add milk, oil, 1¼ cups water, and yeast mixture. Mix well (by hand or using the dough hook attachment on a stand mixer), adding more flour until dough forms into a ball.

Turn out onto a lightly floured work surface and knead for 5 minutes. Divide dough in two pieces.

Lightly oil two large bowls. Place dough in each bowl and turn to coat with oil on all sides. Cover with oiled plastic wrap and set aside for 3 hours, or until doubled.

Punch down dough. Let rise again.

Preheat oven to 400°F. Oil two Dutch ovens.

When dough is doubled, carefully remove from bowls and place in Dutch ovens. (Try not to deflate dough.) Bake covered for 30 minutes, or until brown and bread makes a distinct, hollow, "thump" sound when tapped.

Makes 2 loaves.

My favorite bread. Delicious and unpretentious.
Deborah Lane, Buckhannon, West Virginia

❧ IRISH SODA BREAD ❧

This is the moistest Irish soda bread I've ever had. Toasted, then spread with butter and marmalade, it is magic. From now on, it's the only Irish soda bread I'll make. It's easier and has better texture. One preference: I like my Irish soda bread to have caraway seeds or raisins but not both. Do as you please. –D.T.

1 cup golden raisins or your preference

1 shot or 3 tablespoons plus 1 teaspoon
   Irish whiskey or any dark liquor

4 cups all-purpose flour

¼ cup sugar

1 teaspoon baking soda

1 teaspoon baking powder

1 teaspoon salt

2 eggs

2 cups buttermilk

1 tablespoon melted butter

1 to 2 tablespoons caraway seeds
   (optional)

Preheat oven to 350°F. Grease and lightly flour a loaf or cake pan. If using cast iron, put into cold oven and preheat as oven warms. Grease with butter before putting dough into it.

In a bowl, combine raisins and liquor, set aside to soak, and stir occasionally.

In another bowl, mix together flour, sugar, baking soda, baking powder, and salt.

In a separate bowl, beat together eggs and buttermilk. Add to flour mixture and stir to blend. Add butter, raisins and whiskey, and caraway seeds (if using) and stir.

Pour into prepared pan, smooth to level dough, and bury raisins as much as possible.

Bake for 1 hour and 15 minutes to 1 hour and 30 minutes, or until a toothpick inserted into the center comes out clean. Or, out of pan, check to see if bottom is golden brown. Or tap bread: Hollow sound indicates bread is done. Let cool before wrapping.

Makes 1 loaf.

This recipe comes from my Aunt Rita, from a very long time ago. She wrote at the bottom, "Nobody outside the family has this recipe. There are many variations but not the same. Even a baker from Ireland asked for it but he didn't get it." Coming from a very large Irish family, we have always celebrated St. Patrick's Day, with the Grey Corned Beef and cabbage and all the fixings to the Irish step dancing that would always take place in the home. I have made some adjustments to this recipe, but only to soaking the raisins in the Jameson!

Maureen Marino, Amherst, Massachusetts

❦ STRAWBERRY BREAD ❧

A delicious tea bread that is extremely moist and full of flavor. I brought one to a family gathering, gifted another to a friend, and enjoyed the third smeared with strawberry cream cheese. –S.L.P.

1 cup (2 sticks) butter, softened

1½ cups sugar

1 teaspoon vanilla extract

¼ teaspoon lemon extract

4 eggs

3 cups all-purpose flour

1 teaspoon salt

1 teaspoon cream of tartar

½ teaspoon baking soda

1 cup strawberry preserves

1 cup chopped walnuts

½ cup sour cream

Preheat oven to 350°F. Grease three 8x4-inch loaf pans.

In a bowl, cream butter, sugar, vanilla, and lemon extract until soft. Add eggs, one at a time, beating well after each addition.

In another bowl, sift together flour, salt, cream of tartar, and baking soda.

In a separate bowl, combine preserves, nuts, and sour cream. Add preserves mixture and dry ingredients alternately to butter mixture. Pour into prepared pans.

Bake for 50 minutes, or until a tester inserted into the center comes out clean. Cool on racks for 10 minutes before removing from pans to cool completely.

Makes 3 loaves.

Almanac favorite

Cream of tartar (potassium hydrogen tartrate) is what is left over after juice from grapes has been fermented into wine.

ℒ ZUCCHINI BREAD ℛ

TESTER'S COMMENTS

This loaf is one of the best reasons never to say "no" to fresh zucchini offered by a gardening neighbor or friend. A lightly toasted and buttered slice—if you can eat just one—is out of this world. This recipe makes two loaves, which is good in case you want to put one into the freezer for when unexpected company comes—or you find that you simply can't stop eating it. –S.L.P.

3 cups all-purpose flour

1¼ teaspoons salt

1 teaspoon baking soda

1 teaspoon ground cinnamon

¼ teaspoon baking powder

2 cups sugar

1 cup vegetable oil

3 eggs

2 cups unpeeled, shredded zucchini, drained well

2 teaspoons vanilla extract

½ teaspoon lemon zest

½ cup chopped nuts (optional)

Preheat oven to 325°F. Grease and flour two 9x5-inch loaf pans.

In a bowl, sift together flour, salt, baking soda, cinnamon, and baking powder.

In another bowl, combine sugar, oil, and eggs. Add zucchini, vanilla, lemon zest, and nuts (if using) and stir to blend well. Add dry ingredients and stir to just combine.

Pour batter into prepared pans. Bake for 60 minutes, or until a toothpick inserted into the center comes out clean. Cool in pans for 10 minutes, then turn out onto a rack to cool.

Makes 2 loaves.

This recipe has hung around for 37 years. I can't remember where I got it (maybe a swim instructor?), but now it's definitely a family favorite. You can bake it for brunch or potlucks and it's an easy and appreciated "thank you" gift, teacher gift, "thinking of you" gift, holiday gift—you name it! I'd add only that it sometimes tastes better the second day, so you can make ahead. Everyone likes it, and it doesn't taste like zucchini bread; often it's a "secret" ingredient that I share only afterward to surprise people.

Beth Fitzgerald, Williamsburg, Ohio

❧ PERSIMMON BREAD ❧

TESTER'S COMMENTS

Of all my recipe tests, this was the most mysterious. I had never eaten anything with persimmon and neither had the tasters. The brandy is subtle; few tasters noticed it, and they were surprised to learn that it was an ingredient. A couple suggested using fewer raisins. But everyone loved the taste and texture of this fruit cake-y loaf. "It's a holiday cake," said several. –L.R.

3½ cups all-purpose flour

2½ cups sugar

2 teaspoons baking soda

1½ teaspoons salt

1 teaspoon ground nutmeg

2 cups puréed persimmons (4 to 5 fruit)

1 cup (2 sticks) melted unsalted butter

4 eggs, at room temperature

⅔ cup brandy

2 cups chopped walnuts, or other nuts

2 cups raisins, or other dried fruit

Preheat oven to 350°F. Butter two loaf pans and dust with flour.

In a bowl, mix together flour, sugar, baking soda, salt, and nutmeg. Make a well in the center.

In another bowl, mix together persimmon purée, butter, eggs, and brandy. Add to well and stir to blend. Add nuts and raisins and stir.

Pour into prepared pans. Bake for 1 hour, or until a toothpick inserted into the center comes out clean.

Makes 2 loaves.

When we bought our property, we found that we had a persimmon tree. This tree creates a bounty of fruit. However, the fruit is very bitter and calls for quite a bit of sugar. Over the years, I have perfected this recipe and often make it for neighbors and friends during the holidays. It also freezes well.

Shara Bleakley, Conroe, Texas

The Latin name for the persimmon genus, *Diospyros,* means "food of the gods."

BREADS: SWEET

DESSERTS

❧ SIMPLE SIMON CAKE ❧

Easy enough for kids to make; moist and chocolate-y enough for adults to love. The glossy surface of this cake is "frosting" enough, but if you must, add a dab of whipped cream or yogurt. Just don't expect this treat to last long. –C.S.

1½ cups sifted all-purpose flour

1 cup sugar

¼ cup unsweetened cocoa powder

1 teaspoon baking soda

½ teaspoon salt

5 tablespoons vegetable oil

1 teaspoon vanilla extract

1 teaspoon apple cider vinegar

1½ cups applesauce, canned or homemade
  (see below)

Preheat oven to 350°F. Grease an 8x8-inch baking dish.

Sift flour, sugar, cocoa, baking soda, and salt together into prepared pan. Make three impressions in dry ingredients. Pour oil into one, vanilla into second, and vinegar into third. Spread applesauce all over. Mix well until smooth. Bake for 25 to 30 minutes, or until a toothpick inserted into the center comes out clean. Cool before serving.

Makes 8 servings.

My mother used to make this for us. I am glad to have her recipe and happy to share it.

David Hearn, Bloomington, Illinois

HOW TO MAKE APPLESAUCE

Peel and core 5 to 6 apples and cut into large slices.

Put apples into an enamel pan with 1 cup water and a dash of lemon juice.

Bring to a boil then reduce heat and simmer for 30 minutes.

Remove from heat and stir to break up apples.

Taste and add sugar, if desired.

DESSERTS: CAKES

❧ WALDORF CAKE ❧

This cake is almost too pretty to eat—but it didn't stop tasters! The cake was moist with a subtle hint of chocolate, and the not-too-sweet icing was the perfect complement. –S.L.P.

Cake:

1 tablespoon white vinegar

1 teaspoon baking soda

1½ cups sugar

½ cup shortening

2 eggs

2 tablespoons unsweetened cocoa powder

1 ounce red food coloring

2¼ cups cake flour (see below)

1 cup buttermilk

1 teaspoon salt

1 teaspoon vanilla extract

Icing:

1 cup milk

3 tablespoons all-purpose flour

1 cup (2 sticks) butter

1 cup sugar

1 teaspoon vanilla extract

For cake: Preheat oven to 350°F. Grease and flour two 9-inch cake pans.

In a bowl, combine vinegar and baking soda and set aside.

In another bowl, cream sugar and shortening, then stir in eggs. Make a paste using cocoa and food coloring, then add to sugar mixture. Alternately add flour and buttermilk to sugar mixture, stirring well after each addition. Stir in salt and vanilla. Stir in vinegar mixture.

Pour batter into prepared pans. Bake for 30 minutes, or until a toothpick inserted into the center comes out clean.

For icing: Put milk and flour into a jar and shake to combine. Pour into a saucepan over medium-low heat and cook until thick. Cover, remove from heat, and cool.

In a bowl, cream butter and sugar, then add vanilla and stir until fluffy. Add cooled milk mixture, blending very lightly and briefly.

To assemble: Slice cooled layers in half horizontally. Place one layer on a cake plate. Spread icing on top. Repeat with other layers.

Makes 8 servings.

This recipe has been in my mother's family for generations. Many call this red velvet cake, but the icing makes it very unique and different from typical red velvet cakes. I make this for most of our family and holiday dinners and as birthday gifts for my sisters.

Malea Jessen, Macomb, Illinois

HOW TO MAKE CAKE FLOUR

For every 1 cup of cake flour needed, measure 1 cup of all-purpose flour and remove 3 tablespoons.
Add 3 tablespoons of cornstarch to the all-purpose flour and sift several times.

THIRD-GENERATION BANANA CAKE WITH CHOCOLATE FROSTING

Banana lovers have a fancy alternative to familiar banana bread with this recipe. The cake is light, much different from a traditional banana loaf, and the frosting is like a candy bar. –C.S.

Cake:

1½ cups sugar

½ cup shortening

2 eggs, slightly beaten

1 teaspoon vanilla extract

2¼ cups all-purpose flour

2½ teaspoons baking powder

½ teaspoon baking soda

½ teaspoon salt

¼ cup sour milk (mix ½ teaspoon white vinegar in milk)

4 very ripe bananas, mashed well

Frosting:

2 cups sugar

½ cup (1 stick) butter

½ cup unsweetened cocoa powder

½ cup milk

pinch of salt

For cake: Preheat oven to 350°F.

In a bowl, cream sugar and shortening. Add eggs and vanilla and mix well.

In another bowl, sift together flour, baking powder, baking soda, and salt. Add to sugar mixture alternately with sour milk and bananas. Mix well.

Pour into a 13x9-inch baking pan. Bake for 30 to 35 minutes, or until a toothpick inserted into the center comes out clean. Cool completely.

For frosting: Prepare an ice bath (fill kitchen sink with cold water and ice cubes).

In a saucepan, combine sugar, butter, cocoa, milk, and salt. Cook over medium heat until boiling, stirring constantly. Place pan immediately into ice bath, deep enough for water to come halfway up side of pan. Stir frosting constantly for 2 to 3 minutes, or until it is thick. Do not splash water into it. Remove from bath and spread on cake.

Makes 10 to 12 servings.

Banana cake with chocolate frosting has been a tradition in our family for about 70 years. It has been passed down through three generations, hence the name. It is by far the family's top choice. We always shared it when we were together, so many memories have been made due to the mutual love of this one dessert.

Betty Gair, Allentown, Pennsylvania

DESSERTS: CAKES

BOSTON CREAM PIE

TESTER'S COMMENTS

Want to see faces light up? Say the three little words "Boston Cream Pie," then bring out this custard-filled and chocolate-frosted classic that is sure to become a family favorite. –C.S.

Cake:

1 cup sifted all-purpose flour

1 teaspoon baking powder

2 eggs

1 cup sugar

1 teaspoon vanilla extract

¼ teaspoon salt

1 tablespoon butter, melted

½ cup boiling milk

Filling:

1 package (3.4 ounces) instant or cook-and-serve vanilla pudding mix

Frosting:

1½ cups confectioners' sugar

¼ cup unsweetened cocoa powder

¼ cup (½ stick) butter, softened

3 tablespoons milk

½ teaspoon vanilla extract

For cake: Preheat oven to 350°F. Grease and flour a 9-inch cake pan.

In a bowl, sift together flour and baking powder.

In another bowl, beat eggs until light. Beat in sugar, vanilla, and salt. Beat in butter, then boiling milk.

Add dry ingredients to egg mixture and beat to just blended.

Pour into prepared cake pan. Bake for 25 to 30 minutes, or until a toothpick inserted into the center comes out clean. Set aside to cool. Remove from pan and slice layer in half horizontally. Place bottom half on a cake plate.

For filling: Prepare pudding according to package directions. Cool, then spread on bottom cake layer.

For frosting: In a bowl, sift together confectioners' sugar and cocoa. Add butter alternately with milk, beating thoroughly. Stir in vanilla.

Transfer to a saucepan. Cook over low heat for 5 minutes, or until dark and glossy, stirring constantly.

To assemble: Place top half of cake on filling. Spread frosting on top of cake, dripping some down the sides. Refrigerate until time to serve.

Makes 8 to 10 servings.

This is from one of the first cookbooks I ever owned, and I still have it from the 1960s. Boston Cream Pie is one of the family favorites, and I have made it so many times that the pages in the old book are stuck together with batter, splattered milk or eggs, and who knows what. I don't need a bookmark; the page is so thick, the book opens right to my favorite recipe. Even though the binding is busted and ripped, just to see this much-loved book is to remember how many times we've enjoyed this recipe, and I hope everyone else enjoys it as much!

Kathy Hiortdahl, Davenport, Florida

❧ HEAVENLY PLUM KUCHEN ❧

TESTER'S COMMENTS

"Heavenly" is right! This brought back memories of my memere's homemade kuchen. –S.L.P.

1 cup sugar
½ cup (1 stick) butter, softened
1¼ cups all-purpose flour
½ teaspoon salt
½ teaspoon ground cinnamon
½ teaspoon baking powder
1 pound fresh plums, halved and pitted
1 egg
1 cup light cream

Preheat oven to 375°F.

In a bowl, cream together sugar and butter.

In another bowl, sift together flour, salt, cinnamon, and baking powder. Combine with butter mixture. Reserve ⅓ cup of mixture.

Press remaining batter evenly into bottom and about 1 inch up sides of a 10-inch pie plate or 8x8-inch baking pan. Arrange plums, rounded side up, in a single layer on batter. Sprinkle with reserved crumb mixture. Bake for 15 minutes.

In a separate bowl, beat egg and stir in cream. Pour over plums. Bake for 30 minutes more, or until custard is set. Serve at room temperature.

Makes 6 to 8 servings.

When I was a child, in mid-1960s, our minister's wife shared this recipe with us. Our whole family loved this creamy, fruity, crunchy dessert. When everyone started getting computers, we transferred the recipe from index card to computer file, and we lost it when our computer crashed. Years later, I did a recipe search for "Heavenly Plum Kuchen"—and lo, I found it online! It just proves that you can find anything on the Internet. Thank you, Marge Kling!

Linda Ruth, Peterborough, New Hampshire

Kuchen (pronounced KOO-ken) is a German cake
usually made with fruit and often served with coffee.

DESSERTS: CAKES

Nana's Apple Pecan Cake

Deliciously moist and loaded with apples, this cake is still easily cut into "clean" slices. —C.S.

DESSERTS: CAKES

2 cups sugar

1½ cups vegetable oil

2 teaspoons vanilla extract

2 eggs

2½ cups sifted all-purpose flour

1 teaspoon salt

1 teaspoon baking soda

1 teaspoon baking powder

1 cup chopped pecans

3 cups peeled, cored, and chopped apples

Preheat oven to 350°F. Grease and flour a tube pan.

In a bowl, combine sugar, oil, vanilla, and eggs. Using an electric mixer, beat on low speed.

In another bowl, sift together flour, salt, baking soda, and baking powder. Add to creamed mixture in small amounts. Beat well after each addition. When batter is stiff, remove beaters and mix by hand. Stir in pecans and apples.

Pour into prepared pan. Bake for 1 hour, or until a toothpick inserted into the center comes out clean. Cake will be golden brown. Cool in pan for 15 minutes. Run knife around pan's inner edge, then cool 10 minutes more. Remove to a cooling rack.

Makes 16 servings.

Every year, my grandmother baked this cake for our family Christmas Eve gathering at her house. When I moved to Colorado, I realized that I didn't have the recipe. I asked Nana to send it to me in December of 1992. I still have the copy in her beautiful handwriting. It is in a protective covering in a three-ring binder that contains my favorite recipes. When I made a recipe binder for my son, I included a copy of the recipe in Nana's handwriting. I will do the same for my granddaughter when she is older. Nana passed away in 2011, but the tradition continues in our family.

Angela Harper, Marcos, Colorado

Keep pecans in an airtight container to prevent them from absorbing odors or other flavors. Store them in the refrigerator for up to 9 months or in the freezer for up to 2 years.

❧ ROCK THE CARROT ❧

TESTER'S COMMENTS

I expected these layers, coated with the glaze, to be extra sweet—but no: The glaze made the cake moist and delicious. This is going into my recipe box for future use as "The Best Carrot Cake." –L.R.

Cake:

2 cups all-purpose flour

2 teaspoons baking soda

2 teaspoons ground cinnamon

½ teaspoon salt

3 eggs

2 cups sugar

¾ cup vegetable oil

¾ cup buttermilk

2 teaspoons vanilla extract

2 cups grated carrots

1 can (8 ounces) crushed pineapple, drained

½ cup sweetened coconut flakes

1 cup chopped pecans or walnuts

Buttermilk glaze:

1 cup sugar

½ cup buttermilk

½ cup (1 stick) butter

1 tablespoon light corn syrup

1½ teaspoons baking soda

1 teaspoon vanilla extract

Cream cheese frosting:

¾ cup (1½ sticks) butter, softened

1 package (8 ounces) cream cheese, softened

3 cups sifted confectioners' sugar

1½ teaspoons vanilla extract

pecans or walnuts, for garnish (optional)

Preheat oven to 350°F. Line three 9-inch cake pans with wax paper. Lightly grease and flour wax paper.

For cake: In a bowl, combine flour, baking soda, cinnamon, and salt.

In another bowl, combine eggs, sugar, oil, buttermilk, and vanilla. Using an electric mixer, beat until smooth. Add flour mixture, beating at low speed until blended. Fold in carrots, pineapple, coconut, and pecans by hand.

Pour batter evenly into prepared cake pans. Bake for 25 to 30 minutes, or until a toothpick inserted into the center comes out clean.

For buttermilk glaze: In a heavy-bottom saucepan, combine sugar, buttermilk, butter, corn syrup, and

baking soda. Bring to a boil over medium-high heat. Boil for 4 minutes, stirring often. Remove from heat and stir in vanilla.

Drizzle glaze evenly over top of each warm layer. Cool in pans on wire racks for 15 minutes. Remove from pans and cool completely on wire racks.

For cream cheese frosting: In a bowl, beat together butter and cream cheese until creamy. Add confectioners' sugar and vanilla and beat until smooth.

To assemble: Place one layer on a cake plate. Spread frosting on top, followed by another layer. Repeat. Frost top and sides. Decorate with pecans (if using).

Makes 8 to 10 servings.

This was my father's favorite. Unfortunately, my mother would make it only in springtime. We would all hover around the kitchen with forks in hand to get that first piece. I have tried to keep the tradition going, but I bake this throughout the year. Be prepared—your company will want seconds!

Jen Smallwood, Portsmouth, Virginia

❧ ALMOND CHEESECAKE ❧

This is a great dessert option for people with gluten allergies. It's very easy to make. What's more, it looks wonderful. Although the almond extract succumbs to the vanilla, the taste is pleasing—at least one taster compared it to rich ice cream. To add pizzazz, put fresh seasonal berries on top or serve with each slice. –D.T.

3 packages (8 ounces each) cream cheese, softened
5 eggs
1 cup plus 4 tablespoons sugar, divided
¼ teaspoon almond extract
2 cups sour cream
1 teaspoon vanilla extract

Preheat oven to 325°F. Grease a 10-inch pie plate.

In a bowl, beat cream cheese until light and creamy. Add eggs, one at a time, beating after each. Add 1 cup sugar and almond extract. Beat for 5 minutes, or until smooth, thick, and lemon-color.

Pour into prepared plate. Bake for 50 minutes. Cool for 20 minutes.

In a bowl, beat together sour cream, remaining 4 tablespoons sugar, and vanilla. Drop by spoonfuls onto cheesecake and spread smooth. Bake for 15 minutes more. Cool, then refrigerate for 24 to 48 hours before cutting.

Makes 8 to 12 servings.

When I got out of nurses' training in Peoria, Illinois, in 1963, my girlfriend and I flew out to Long Beach, California, to work at the Veterans' Administration Hospital for a couple of years. We lived at an apartment complex that had lots of young people from many different areas. One of the girls out there gave me this recipe. I think it is like New York cheesecake. It is so easy to make. You don't have to use a springform pan—just a glass pie plate. And you don't have to worry about a crust; the filling forms its own crust. I have taken this cheesecake to work and to many family meals, and all of my sisters now have the recipe. They call it Nancy's Cheesecake.

Nancy Reed, Elmwood, Illinois

❧ MIKE'S CHEESECAKE ❧

TESTER'S COMMENTS

The beauty of this recipe is its versatility: graham cracker crust, your favorite piecrust, or no crust. I used a refrigerator piecrust, rolled to fit my 2-quart dish and baked per the package directions. Instead of canned fruit, I used fresh strawberries. After the cheesecake had cooked for 1 hour, I put the berries on top and baked the cake until the berries started to caramelize—a few minutes. Meanwhile, I heated strawberry jelly on low on the stovetop. This I brushed on the berries when the cheesecake came out of the oven. After letting it cool for 30 minutes, I chilled it. This is a rich, dense, cheesecake that does indeed melt in your mouth. –C.S.

Crust:

graham cracker or pie dough crust, or no crust

Filling:

4 packages (8 ounces each) cream cheese, softened

1 cup sugar

2 eggs (more make it lighter and less cream-cheesy)

dash of vanilla extract

Topping:

fresh fruit or 1 can (20 ounces) of your favorite fruit pie filling

Preheat oven to 275°F.

For crust (if using): Press prepared graham cracker crust or rolled out pie dough into bottom and sides of 9x9-inch glass baking dish.

For filling: In a bowl, combine cream cheese, sugar, eggs, and vanilla and beat thoroughly. Pour into prepared crust or crustless glass baking dish. Bake for 1 hour, or until top is golden.

For topping: Spread fruit on top. Return cheesecake to oven to bake until the sugar in the fruit starts to caramelize. Cool, then refrigerate until cold.

Makes 8 to 10 servings.

I love cheesecake, so when I saw, 25 years ago, that cream cheese was on sale, I decided to make one. I checked my cookbooks for a recipe and found several, but they all had ricotta or other cheeses in addition to cream cheese, which did not sound good to me, so I decided to wing it. For the first cheesecake, I patted a traditional graham cracker crust along the bottom and sides of a rectangular glass baking dish, but I later used a regular pie crust (which I prefer). Then I tried it with no crust at all and found that the cheese hardened along the bottom and sides of the dish to make a yummy cream cheese crust. Plus, without a crust, it has less calories. The recipe I invented gave me the perfect cheesecake. It was rich, creamy, and heavy, exactly the way I wanted it to be. You are guaranteed the heaviest, creamiest cheesecake ever. For maximum heavenliness, place a spoonful on your tongue and just let it sit there and slowly dissolve.

Michael Steinberg, State College, Pennsylvania

GRILLED ANGEL FOOD CAKE WITH BERRY-WINE SAUCE & FRESH LEMON WHIPPED CREAM

TESTER'S COMMENTS

The combination of flavors is brilliant: The spiced wine sauce tastes like Christmas, while the berries and lemony whipped cream evoke early summer, like sophisticated shortcake. Feel free to fiddle with the grilling. I tried a cast-iron stovetop grill pan, a cast-iron skillet, and untoasted. Grilled with the marks is the prettiest. –D.T.

Sauce:

1 cup sugar

1 cup good cabernet wine

1 cinnamon stick

orange rind stuck with 4 cloves

2 pounds (about 7½ cups) strawberries, hulled and sliced

Whipped cream:

1 cup whipping cream

3 tablespoons confectioners' sugar

1 tablespoon lemon zest

1 tablespoon fresh lemon juice

1 teaspoon vanilla extract

Cake

1 angel food cake (favorite homemade recipe or prepared), sliced

sliced strawberries (optional)

mint sprigs (optional)

For sauce: In a saucepan, combine sugar, wine, cinnamon stick, and orange rind with cloves. Bring to a boil. Simmer for 30 minutes, or until reduced by half, stirring occasionally. Strain out cinnamon stick, orange rind, and cloves. Cool, then pour over sliced berries and stir to coat. Chill in refrigerator.

For whipped cream: In a bowl, beat whipping cream until foamy. Gradually add confectioners' sugar, lemon zest, lemon juice, and vanilla. Continue whipping until soft peaks form.

To assemble: Preheat grill to medium. Spray angel food cake slices with cooking spray. Grill on each side for a couple of minutes, or until grill marks appear and slices are golden brown.

Place each cake slice on a serving dish. Spoon berry sauce over. Top with dollop of whipped cream. Garnish with fresh berries and mint (if using).

Makes 8 servings.

I entered this recipe in a local EyeCook Contest and it won third place in desserts. The sauce is the star in this favorite. Wonderfully versatile, with rave reviews from family and friends!

Jena Lords, Bakersfield, California

Orange Pecan Cake

TESTER'S COMMENTS

This cake is moist, tender, and a mouthful of sunshine! If its aroma fills the air, check for doneness. The orange pulp adds a gooey chew, while the pecans add crunch. The fresh juice glaze provides all of the sweetness needed. –J.S.

1 juicer orange (such as navel or Valencia)
½ cup (1 stick) butter, softened
1¾ cups sugar, divided
2 eggs
1 cup light cream
1 tablespoon fresh lemon juice
2 cups sifted all-purpose flour
1 teaspoon baking soda
¼ teaspoon salt
¾ cup roughly chopped pecans
¼ cup fresh orange juice

Preheat oven to 375°F. Butter and flour an 8x8-inch baking dish.

Cut unpeeled orange into eighths (or smaller) and remove any seeds. Reduce to pulp in a blender or food processor.

In a bowl, cream butter, gradually adding 1½ cups sugar a little at a time. Beat until light and fluffy. Add orange pulp and mix well. Add eggs, one at a time, beating well after each.

In another bowl, combine cream and lemon juice.

In a separate bowl, sift together flour, baking soda, and salt. Add to orange mixture alternately with cream mixture. Mix well. Gently stir in nuts.

Spread in prepared dish. Bake for 45 minutes, or until a toothpick inserted into the center comes out clean. Immediately sprinkle with remaining ¼ cup sugar, then pour orange juice over to glaze.

Makes 8 servings.

My aunt and I came up with this recipe about 50 years ago as a way to use the oranges from our trees. I have been enjoying it and making it for friends and family for all these years.

R. Cohen, Longboat Key, Florida

If you forget to soften your butter, cut the stick(s) into thin pats and place them on a plate. Leave the plate in a warm spot for 10 minutes or so, until the butter yields to gentle finger pressure.

PINEAPPLE UPSIDE-DOWN CAKE WITH RASPBERRIES

I've never been a pineapple upside-down cake kind of gal, but the sweet, sticky sauce combined with the rather plain cake had me back for seconds. –D.T.

Up side:

¼ cup (½ stick) butter, for pan

½ cup packed brown sugar

1 can (20 ounces) pineapple slices, drained, juice reserved

fresh raspberries

Cake:

1 cup sugar

½ cup (1 stick) butter, at room temperature

3 eggs

½ cup sour cream

1 cup whole wheat flour

½ cup unbleached white flour

1 teaspoon baking powder

½ teaspoon baking soda

¼ teaspoon salt

Glaze:

reserved pineapple juice

¼ cup sugar

2 tablespoons (¼ stick) butter

Preheat oven to 350°F.

For up side: Smear butter inside a 9-inch cake pan, especially on bottom. Sprinkle brown sugar on bottom. Arrange pineapple slices in a single layer on brown sugar. Place 1 raspberry between and inside each pineapple ring.

For cake: In a bowl, beat sugar with butter until creamy. Add eggs, one at a time, beating after each. Add sour cream and mix well.

In another bowl, mix flours, baking powder, baking soda, and salt. Add to butter mixture and stir until dry ingredients are just incorporated.

Pour batter over pineapple slices. Bake for 40 to 50 minutes, turning pan halfway through, or until a toothpick inserted into the center comes out clean. Lightly cover top with aluminum foil to keep from browning, if necessary.

For glaze: Pour reserved pineapple juice into a saucepan. Add sugar and butter. Cook over low heat, stirring, until liquid is reduced by about half. Keep warm.

Cool cake on a rack for 5 to 10 minutes. Loosen sides with a knife and turn cake out onto a serving plate. Pour glaze over top. Serve warm or cool.

Makes 8 to 10 servings.

Gluten-free flour can be substituted for whole wheat and unbleached white flours. I love this cake, and it is my son's favorite birthday cake.

Catia, Redway, California

STICKY TOFFEE PUDDING WITH BUTTERSCOTCH SAUCE

This luscious pudding cake took tasters by surprise. Everyone should try it at least once. For individual puddings, divide batter into six ramekins and bake for 30 minutes, or until a toothpick inserted into the center comes out clean. –J.S.

Pudding:

¾ cup superfine sugar

¼ cup (½ stick) unsalted butter

1 teaspoon vanilla extract

2 eggs

1⅓ cups scone flour (see below)

6 ounces dates, finely chopped

1 teaspoon baking soda

Sauce:

¾ cup packed dark brown sugar

½ cup superfine sugar

½ cup (1 stick) unsalted butter

1¼ cups dark corn syrup

1 cup heavy cream

whipped cream or ice cream (optional)

For pudding: Preheat oven to 300°F. Butter and flour an 8x6x2-inch baking dish or casserole.

In a bowl, combine sugar, butter, and vanilla. Using an electric mixer, beat on low until well mixed and creamy in color. Add eggs, one at a time, beating well after each. Fold flour into mixture.

Bring 1 cup water to a boil in a saucepan, add dates, return to boiling, and cook for 2 minutes. Remove from heat and add baking soda (adding it when mixture is on heat will cause it to rush over top of pan). Add dates and water to batter and mix well.

Pour into prepared pan. Bake for 40 to 45 minutes, or until a toothpick inserted into the center comes out clean.

For sauce: In a saucepan, combine sugars, butter, and corn syrup and gently bring to a boil. When it starts to bubble, add cream and return to boiling. Make sure sugars are melted. Keep sauce warm.

Drizzle sauce over pudding. Serve slices drizzled with more sauce. Top with whipped cream (if using).

Makes 9 servings.

I got this recipe about 15 years ago from a British woman in the Cotswolds of England. The "pudding" is actually a very moist sponge cake. In the oven, it looks like a watery mess, but this is what makes the moist, rich, and decadent sponge cake. It's something different during the holidays or anytime—and it's why my family goes on long walks after a big holiday feast!

Catherine Boeckmann, Indianapolis, Indiana

HOW TO MAKE SCONE FLOUR

Sift together 1 pound all-purpose flour with ⅛ cup baking powder.

❧ SALTED CARAMEL "APPLE CHARLOTTE" ❧

This is distinctly, deliciously different, with or without the topping. –J.S.

Charlotte:

½ loaf French or firm white bread to yield 4 cups soft bread crumbs

¼ cup (½ stick) butter

½ cup brown sugar

1 tablespoon lemon zest

1 teaspoon ground cinnamon

½ teaspoon ground nutmeg

½ teaspoon finely grated crystallized ginger

4 cups peeled, cored, and thinly sliced apples

1 tablespoon fresh lemon juice

½ cup apricot jam

Topping:

½ cup whipping cream

2 tablespoons confectioners' sugar

1 tablespoon rum or brandy (optional)

½ cup caramel ice cream topping

sea salt

For Charlotte: Remove crusts from bread and allow slices to dry out. Tear bread into pieces and place in food processor. Pulse until crumbs are pea-size.

Melt butter in a skillet over medium heat and toast crumbs until golden brown.

In a bowl, combine brown sugar, lemon zest, cinnamon, nutmeg, and ginger.

In another bowl, combine apples and lemon juice.

Warm jam in microwave (25 to 30 seconds, medium power) to make easier to spread.

To assemble: Preheat oven to 350°F. Generously butter sides and bottom of 8-inch casserole or springform baking pan.

Spread 1½ cups bread crumbs on bottom of prepared pan. Cover with half of apple slices. Sprinkle with one-third of brown sugar mixture. Spread half of apricot jam on top. (Pastry brush or soft spatula works well.) Repeat with 1½ cups bread crumbs, remaining apples, one-third of brown sugar mixture, and remaining apricot jam. Combine remaining bread crumbs and remaining one-third of brown sugar mixture. Sprinkle on top. Bake for 35 to 40 minutes, or until lightly browned.

For topping: In a bowl, whip cream with confectioners' sugar and brandy (if using), until stiff peaks form.

To serve: Cut Charlotte into slices and top each slice with whipped cream, caramel sauce (warmed, if desired), and a pinch of sea salt.

Makes 6 to 8 servings.

I was raised in a large family. If there was leftover bread or apples, we knew we could count on bread pudding, an apple pie, or Apple Charlotte. I use my mom's recipe and update it with caramel and apricot jam. I've also made it with pears instead of apples, and other jams. The best part of making it now is that I get to eat it all without having to share!

Darlene Buerger, Peoria, Arizona

DESSERTS: CAKES

APPLE PIE WITH GLUTEN-FREE CHEDDAR CHEESE CRUST

TESTER'S COMMENTS

Baking gluten-free is an art and takes some practice, for sure. This crust may be a challenge for those not accustomed to it. Gluten-free flour has a different feel (and a different chemical reaction) than wheat flour. Adding cheese to the flour mixture is brilliant! My crust looked flaky but may be an acquired taste. However, the filling is excellent and plentiful. –C.S.

Crust:

2½ cups all-purpose gluten-free flour

2½ cups coarsely shredded extra- or medium-sharp cheddar cheese (preferably white)

½ teaspoon salt

¾ cup (1½ sticks) cold unsalted butter, cut into ½-inch pieces

½ cup ice water (sometimes more)

1 tablespoon milk, for glaze

Filling:

12 to 14 apples (a mix of tart and sweet varieties), peeled, cored, and sliced (leave some big chunks)

½ to ¾ cup brown sugar

3 tablespoons all-purpose gluten-free flour

3 tablespoons fresh lemon juice

½ teaspoon ground cinnamon, plus more for sprinkling

¼ teaspoon ground ginger

¼ teaspoon ground nutmeg

¼ teaspoon salt

pinch of ground cloves, or to taste

pinch of ground cardamom, or to taste

4 tablespoons (½ stick) cold unsalted butter, cut into small pieces

milk, for brushing

sugar, for sprinkling

For crust: In a bowl, combine flour, cheese, and salt. Add butter and work with fingertips just until mixture resembles coarse meal, with some roughly pea-size butter lumps. Drizzle with ice water and gently incorporate by hand. Do not overwork dough, or it will become tough. (If dough doesn't hold together, add more ice water, 1 tablespoon at a time, until dough takes shape.) Turn out dough onto a work surface and divide in half. Form each half into a 5- to 6-inch disk. Wrap in plastic wrap and chill until firm, at least 1 hour.

Bring each dough disk to room temperature for 10 to 15 minutes before rolling.

Line a baking sheet with aluminum foil and place in middle of oven (to apply heat to bottom crust at beginning of baking and prevent sogginess). Preheat oven to 450°F.

For filling: In a bowl, combine apples, brown sugar, flour, lemon juice, cinnamon, ginger, nutmeg, salt, cloves, and cardamom. Toss to coat.

DESSERTS: PIES & PUDDINGS

Roll out one dough disk on a lightly floured surface with a lightly floured rolling pin. Gently transfer to a 9-inch pie plate. Leave extra dough hanging over side.

Transfer half of filling to shell and dot with half of small butter pieces. Add remaining filling and dot with remaining butter. (If using a pie bird, place in center of filling, with head 1 to 2 inches above.)

Roll out remaining dough. Cover filling. Trim edges, leaving ½-inch overhang. Press edges together to seal (use fork for texture), then fold under. Lightly brush top crust with milk. If not using pie bird, cut five 1-inch-long vents in crust. Sprinkle crust with sugar and cinnamon. Bake on hot baking sheet for 20 minutes. Reduce heat to 375°F. Bake for 40 minutes more, or until crust is golden brown and filling is bubbling. Cool for 2 to 3 hours.

Makes 8 servings.

Before I could even see over the counter, I was baking apple pies with my mom. Every fall I hunt down my favorite variety, Stayman Winesap, and bake, can, and preserve to get me through the year. I don't care how many fancy-schmancy desserts you throw my way; nothing beats apple pie in my book for breakfast, lunch, and dinner. I sadly thought that apple pie would be lost to me forever when I was diagnosed with celiac disease and had to eat gluten-free. My friend Lily Hetzler inspired me to experiment with a gluten-free piecrust and fill it with cheddar cheese. Magic.

Mary Ann Rounseville, Brooklyn, New York

PIE TIPS

Gluten-free flours need more water than wheat flours to come together.

Dough can be stored in the freezer for up to 2 months.

Thaw frozen dough completely in the refrigerator. This crust will not take shape if the butter is frozen.

Gluten-free flours are hard to work with; your crust may not look picture perfect before baking. The crust may look like a patchwork quilt before it goes into the oven, but it comes out gorgeous!

Shield edges of crust with aluminum foil or pie shield for protection while baking at lower temperature (375°F).

Different cheeses have different baking times. If cheese is browning too fast when you lower the oven temperature, put foil loosely around the whole crust. Remove for the last 15 to 20 minutes to let crust brown.

Why a pie bird? It allows steam to escape without having the filling boil over. It also redirects moisture from the bottom of the pie, allowing for a crunchier bottom crust.

❧ Momma Reva's Prizewinning Apple Pie ❧

TESTER'S COMMENTS

This is an easy pie to make, with nice flavor. The peanut butter flavor is mild, even with 2 teaspoons (I added more than instructed). As Reva experienced, it's enough to notice that this is no ordinary apple pie. –M.A.J.

1 unbaked 9-inch double piecrust

1 cup sugar

2 tablespoons all-purpose flour

¼ teaspoon salt

¼ teaspoon ground cinnamon, plus more for sprinkling

¼ teaspoon ground ginger

¼ teaspoon ground cloves, plus more for sprinkling

6 Granny Smith apples, peeled, cored, and sliced

1 teaspoon crunchy peanut butter

1 egg white, lightly beaten (optional)

Preheat oven to 450°F. Grease a 9-inch pie plate. Line pie plate with bottom pastry.

In a bowl, mix together sugar, flour, salt, cinnamon, ginger, and cloves. Add apples and stir to coat.

Pour into prepared pie plate. Sprinkle with pinch of cinnamon.

Thinly spread peanut butter on underside of top crust. Place over apple mixture. Pinch top and bottom crusts together. Sprinkle top with a pinch each of cinnamon and cloves. Pierce decoratively with fork. Brush egg white (if using) over crust for glossy finish. Place aluminum foil around edges of crust to prevent excessive browning.

Bake for 15 minutes. Reduce oven temperature to 350°F and bake for 45 minutes more.

Makes 8 servings.

I entered this recipe in a contest conducted by The Apple Institute of New Jersey in 1966, and it won top prize for the very best apple pie in the state of New Jersey. I was the youngest winner—in my early 20s at that time—and held my 1-year-old son Michael in my arms for the photo. Michael has recently turned 50!

Reva Berman, Boynton Beach, Florida

DESSERTS: PIES & PUDDINGS

SECRET BLUEBERRY PIE

1 unbaked 9-inch double piecrust

⅓ cup sugar

2 tablespoons all-purpose flour

2 teaspoons cornstarch

½ teaspoon ground cinnamon (optional)

3 cups blueberries, preferably fresh

1 teaspoon fresh lemon juice

1 tablespoon butter, cut into pieces

1 teaspoon molasses

Preheat oven to 425°F. Line a pie plate with bottom pastry.

Stir together sugar, flour, cornstarch, and cinnamon (if using). Mix in berries.

Pour filling into bottom piecrust. Sprinkle with lemon juice and dot with butter. Drizzle molasses over the top of filling and lick the spoon (part of the secret). Cover with top piecrust and cut slits to vent. Place aluminum foil on pie edges. Bake for 40 minutes, removing foil 15 minutes before done.

Makes 8 servings.

The first blueberry season after my mother-in-law passed away, my father-in-law brought me a basket of freshly picked blueberries and said, "I'd like these back in a pie." I made my first-ever blueberry pie for him, and when I cut into it and served him a slice, it was very loose. My father-in-law said, "This is the best blueberry pie I've ever had." I figured he'd ask someone else the following year. The next year, same scenario: "I'd like these back in a pie." So, I used every trick in the book to make it thicker, and when I served him the first piece, it didn't run all over the place. As a matter of fact, it looked gelled—too thick—and he said, "This is the best blueberry pie I've ever had." Year three: This time, I used my grandmother's secret that she shared with me for making her apple pie—drizzle molasses over the filling before baking. My father-in-law waited for the pie as I cut the first piece for him, and it was perfect. He said, "This is the best blueberry pie I've ever had."

Brenda Young, Manchester, New Hampshire

❧ BACON MAPLE CREAM PIE ☙

TESTER'S COMMENTS

Tasters said that this is like breakfast and dessert in one bite. The custard filling is smooth as silk, the whipped cream gives the pie air, and the bacon adds saltiness and a little texture. –M.A.J.

2¼ cups whole milk

2¼ cups maple syrup, preferably grade B, divided

3 egg yolks

½ cup all-purpose flour

3 tablespoons cornstarch

2½ teaspoons vanilla extract, divided

1 baked single 9-inch piecrust, cooled

1¼ cups whipping cream, chilled

1 tablespoon sugar

4 slices thick-cut bacon

1 teaspoon Dijon-style mustard

freshly ground black pepper, to taste

In a saucepan, whisk together milk, 2 cups maple syrup, and egg yolks.

In a bowl, sift together flour and cornstarch. Gradually whisk flour mixture into milk mixture. Stir in 2 teaspoons vanilla. Heat to boiling, cooking for 8 minutes, or until very thick, stirring constantly.

Pour into prepared crust. Refrigerate.

In another bowl, whip cream with sugar and remaining ½ teaspoon vanilla. Spread over chilled pie. Refrigerate.

Preheat oven to 375°F. Line a rimmed baking sheet with aluminum foil. Set a cooling rack on foil. Arrange bacon slices across rack in rows, not overlapping.

Whisk together remaining ¼ cup maple syrup and mustard.

Generously spoon over bacon. Bake for 12 to 15 minutes. Turn over bacon slices and baste again. Bake for 5 to 10 minutes more, or until bacon reaches desired crispness. Remove from oven and sprinkle with freshly ground black pepper. Set aside for 5 minutes. Coarsely chop cooled bacon. Sprinkle on top of pie.

Makes 6 to 8 servings.

Online friends and I were having a discussion about real maple syrup. Some of my friends from Australia and South Africa were totally unfamiliar with it. Others, who live in the Deep South, were familiar with it but found it horrendously expensive where they are, compared with here in Wisconsin, where it is relatively plentiful. I was trying to describe its unique flavor. Then the conversation drifted to bacon, and I thought . . . hmm . . . bacon and maple syrup. . . . Why not?

Kathy Kexel, Marshfield, Wisconsin

DESSERTS: PIES & PUDDINGS

❦ BUTTER BUTTER NUT NUT PIE ❦

TESTER'S COMMENTS

What's not to like about "velvety butternut squash goodness with a pleasant hint of orange"—one taster's observation? There are a lot of steps here. You can pace yourself by prepping on different days: first the squash, then the piecrust, refrigerating them a day or two, until you're ready to make the filling. –C.S.

Butternut squash purée:

1 butternut squash (about 2 pounds)

3 tablespoons unsalted butter, softened, divided

zest of 1 orange

2 tablespoons honey

pinch of salt

pinch of ground nutmeg

Crust:

½ cup (1 stick) unsalted butter, softened

⅛ cup honey

¾ teaspoon vanilla butternut flavoring

1¼ cups all-purpose flour

½ cup pecan pieces

Filling:

1 can (14 ounces) sweetened condensed milk

2 eggs, slightly beaten

½ teaspoon ground nutmeg

½ teaspoon ground ginger

½ teaspoon freshly ground black pepper

½ teaspoon salt

1 envelope (0.25 ounce) unflavored gelatin

1¼ cups butternut squash purée

Toffee sauce:

2 tablespoons brown sugar

2 tablespoons (¼ stick) unsalted butter

1 tablespoon molasses

1 tablespoon light corn syrup

½ cup half-and-half

whipped cream, for garnish (optional)

For butternut squash purée: Preheat oven to 350°F.

Halve squashes lengthwise. Remove seeds and strings. Rub insides with 1 tablespoon of butter. Bake, skin side down, in a roasting pan, for 30 to 40 minutes, or until fork-tender. Scoop out flesh and place in food processor. Add orange zest, honey, and remaining 2 tablespoons of butter. Process until smooth. Add salt and nutmeg. Pulse to incorporate. Put in a bowl and set aside.

For crust: Preheat oven to 300°F.

In a bowl, beat butter, honey, and vanilla butternut flavoring until light and fluffy. Add flour, ½ cup at a time, beating well after each addition. If dough becomes too stiff to stir, knead in remaining flour by hand. Work in nuts by hand. Pat dough into an ungreased 9-inch deep-dish pie plate. Prick surface with fork. Bake for 30 to 40 minutes, or until lightly browned. Cool completely in plate on a cooling rack.

For filling: In a bowl, combine milk, eggs, nutmeg, ginger, pepper, and salt. Set aside.

Put 2 tablespoons water in a saucepan. Sprinkle with unflavored gelatin and let stand for 1 minute. Cook, stirring, over low heat until gelatin is completely dissolved, about 2 minutes. Add milk mixture and stir to blend. Continue cooking, stirring, until slightly thickened, about 7 minutes. Stir in squash purée and whisk until no lumps remain. Cook 3 minutes more. Remove from heat.

For toffee sauce: In a saucepan, heat brown sugar, butter, molasses, and corn syrup together gently, stirring, until melted or dissolved. Bring to a boil and cook for 2 minutes, stirring constantly. Remove from heat and whisk in half-and-half.

To assemble: Pour toffee sauce into cooled crust. Chill for 30 minutes. Pour squash filling into crust. Chill for 6 hours or until firm. Garnish with whipped cream, if desired.

Makes 8 to 10 servings.

I left the Metro Atlanta suburbs to become a country girl and avid gardener in remote rural Tennessee 6 years ago. My first year, I had a bumper crop of butternut squash, and my identical twin sister Nanci and I developed this recipe to use it up, experimenting with different spices and running several test batches. It's definitely an indulgent, "special occasion" recipe, with a unique blend of flavors.

Allison Mackey, Iron City, Tennessee

If you do not have vanilla butternut flavoring, you can substitute ¼ teaspoon vanilla extract, ¼ teaspoon almond extract, and ¼ teaspoon butter flavoring.

FRESH PUMPKIN PIE

TESTER'S COMMENTS

This makes an excellent pie. If fresh pumpkin is not available, canned will do nicely. –L.R.

1 unbaked 9- or 10-inch piecrust

2 cups fresh or canned pumpkin purée

1 can (12 ounces) evaporated milk

2 eggs, slightly beaten

¼ cup brown sugar

½ cup sugar

1 teaspoon ground cinnamon

½ teaspoon ground ginger

¼ teaspoon ground nutmeg

⅛ teaspoon ground cloves

Preheat oven to 425°F. Line a pie plate with pastry.

In a bowl, combine pumpkin purée, milk, eggs, sugars, cinnamon, ginger, nutmeg, and cloves.

Pour into piecrust. Bake for 15 minutes. Reduce heat to 350°F and bake for 45 minutes more, or until filling is set but still wobbly in center.

Makes 8 servings.

My husband loved pumpkin pies, so why not make a fresh pumpkin pie? I have been making these for over 23 years. I put any leftover purée into a zipper-lock bag and freeze it so that I can have fresh pumpkin pie for Christmas and Easter. I make two pies for all of the holidays.

Edna Schneeberger, Watkins Glen, New York

HOW TO MAKE FRESH PUMPKIN PURÉE
Preheat oven to 325°F. Wash a 3-pound pie pumpkin and cut
in half. Remove seeds. Bake skin side up on a baking sheet for 1 hour.
When cool enough to handle, remove pumpkin flesh and
purée in a blender or food processor.

🐦 SWEET POTATO PIE 🐦

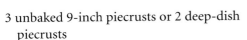

TESTER'S COMMENTS

This is a very good recipe. My third pie, the one with coconut in it, came out great, too. Why not put it in all of them? I would! –L.R.

---

3 unbaked 9-inch piecrusts or 2 deep-dish
   piecrusts

3½ cups mashed cooked sweet potatoes

2 cups sugar

½ cup (1 stick) butter or margarine, melted

4 eggs

1 can (12 ounces) evaporated milk

1 teaspoon vanilla extract

½ teaspoon ground allspice

½ teaspoon salt

⅔ cup sweetened coconut flakes (optional)

Preheat oven to 425°F. Line pie plates with pastry.

Beat sweet potatoes until smooth. Stir in sugar and butter. Beat in eggs, one at a time. Add milk, vanilla, allspice, and salt.

Pour into unbaked piecrusts. (If desired, before pouring third pie, stir in shredded coconut.)

Bake for 20 minutes. Reduce heat to 325°F and bake for 45 minutes more, or until a toothpick inserted into the center comes out clean.

These pies freeze very well.

Makes 3 regular or 2 deep-dish pies.

This is the best pie ever, handed down through several generations. I have wonderful memories of it and of a story about these pies. Every Christmas is memorable; one in particular concerns Mama's holiday baking. She always started her cooking 2 or 3 days ahead because there was so much to do. Mama always made three sweet potato pies, along with three kinds of cakes. We weren't allowed to touch anything until Christmas Eve dinner. Well, one year when Daddy started to eat a piece of sweet potato pie, he noticed that something tasted a little different. Of course, then everyone had to have a taste. We kept tasting and speculating until Mama finally went into the kitchen and took a look around. She came back with a disgusted look on her face. It seems that in her haste to get her cooking done on time, she had put Watkins liniment in the pies instead of vanilla. Well, the liniment bottle looked a lot like the vanilla bottle, and they were about the same size. It seems that the Watkins salesman had been in a liniment sales contest and Daddy had stocked up. A bottle had been left on the kitchen side table. We all had a good laugh, and, needless to say, the pies were still edible. The amount of liniment was so small that it didn't take away from the flavor enough to count—it was just enough to make another Christmas memory.

Cathy Denton, Middlesex, North Carolina

☙ NANA'S FUNNY CAKE ❧

This is a fun "cake" to make. It's in a piecrust, and the chocolate that tops the mixture seeps into the bottom so that there is a chocolate-y layer on the piecrust and a crunchy chocolate layer on the top. The recipe is easy to cut in half for one pie, but why deny yourself an extra one? –C.S.

2 unbaked 9-inch piecrusts

Cake:

2 cups all-purpose flour

1½ cups sugar

1 cup milk

½ cup (1 stick) soft butter or shortening

2 teaspoons baking powder

¼ teaspoon salt

2 eggs

Topping:

1 cup sugar

¾ cup hot water

½ cup unsweetened cocoa powder

½ teaspoon vanilla extract

Preheat oven to 350°F. Line pie plates with pastry.

For cake: In a bowl, combine flour, sugar, milk, butter, baking powder, salt, and eggs.

Pour half into each piecrust.

For topping: In a bowl, combine sugar, hot water, cocoa powder, and vanilla.

Pour half of filling over each pie. Bake for 40 minutes, or until a toothpick inserted into the center comes out clean.

Makes 2 pies.

My mother-in-law made this Pennsylvania Dutch recipe for years. She brought it to the family cabin whenever we spent weekends there together, and it has always been a family favorite! She shared the recipe with me when I got married, along with some of her other wonderful recipes. It continues to be a requested dessert.

Mary Lou Knauss, Duncannon, Pennsylvania

When buying sticks of shortening, note that they do
not come in the same measurements as butter. One stick of butter
equals ½ cup, but one stick of shortening equals 1 cup.

MYRL'S RAISIN PIE

TESTER'S COMMENTS

When I told friends that I had made a raisin pie, reactions were solidly skeptical. Then they tasted it, and reactions were solidly good. The raisins are soft and plump, and they float in vanilla pudding. "Heavenly good," one person said. "Really sweet," said another. (For less sweetness, reduce sugar to 1 cup, using two ½ cups where ¾ cups are indicated.) –D.T.

2½ cups raisins

1½ cups sugar, divided

½ cup (1 stick) butter

4 tablespoons cornstarch

3 eggs

1 cup milk

2 tablespoons vanilla extract

2 frozen piecrusts in pans

Preheat oven to 350°F.

In a saucepan, combine raisins, ¾ cup of sugar, and 1½ cups water. Cook over medium heat for 15 minutes, or until tender. Add butter and stir until melted.

In a bowl, mix together remaining ¾ cup of sugar and cornstarch. Add eggs, milk, and vanilla. Stirring constantly, add small amount of hot raisin mixture to egg mixture. Then slowly add egg mixture to saucepan, continuing to stir. Cook until thick.

Pour into cold piecrusts and bake for 30 minutes, or until crust is brown and the center only gently moves when you jiggle the pie.

Makes 2 pies.

My grandmother, Myrl, was a great cook and a great lady. She loved to feed everyone, and it especially made her happy to make my dad, Willard, his favorite pie—Raisin Pie. As her son-in-law, he loved her dearly but loved to tease her, and she loved it when she made her raisin pie and he oohed-and-aahed. So much love in this recipe!

Lana Brookshire, Maryville, Tennessee

DESSERTS: PIES & PUDDINGS

GRANDMA'S GOOD RHUBARB PIE

TESTER'S COMMENTS

This is good, like a custard pie. I made it with a top crust, but next time I'll try it without one. –L.R.

1 unbaked 9-inch piecrust (a double crust will make a pretty pie)

1 cup all-purpose flour

1 cup sugar

1½ teaspoons salt

3 eggs

3 tablespoons fresh lemon juice

2 teaspoons butter, softened

6 cups chopped rhubarb

Preheat oven to 425°F. Line a pie plate with pastry.

In a bowl, combine flour, sugar and salt.

In another bowl, beat eggs. Add lemon juice and butter and stir to blend. Add to flour mixture and stir to blend. Add rhubarb and mix thoroughly.

Pour into piecrust. Bake for 10 minutes, then reduce heat to 375°F and bake for 45 minutes more.

Makes 6 to 8 servings.

This recipe almost has no business being called "Grandma's." I have no fond childhood memories of her baking it for me; in fact, she hated cooking. She gets her name on it for her remarkable talent of finding and passing on really good recipes.

Dariana Travis, Peterborough, New Hampshire

When you have an excess of rhubarb, freeze it. Choose firm, tender, well-colored stalks. Wash, trim, and cut into 1- to 2-inch pieces. Blanch the rhubarb in boiling water for 1 minute. Cool promptly in cold water to retain color and flavor. Drain well, then pack in a container or plastic freezer bag before freezing.

APPLE GINGERBREAD COBBLER

Ginger and gingerbread are two of my favorites. The batter comes together very easily and when baked makes a firm cake top on a puddinglike bottom. Consider serving it warm, with ginger ice cream—but even without it, you're bound to get raves. –C.S.

---

4 cooking apples, peeled, cored, and sliced

⅓ cup packed brown sugar

1 tablespoon butter

1¼ cups all-purpose flour

1¼ teaspoons baking soda

½ teaspoon ground ginger

¼ teaspoon ground cloves

¼ teaspoon salt

¼ cup shortening

¼ cup sugar

1 egg

⅓ cup molasses

½ cup hot water

Preheat oven to 350°F. Grease a 1½-quart baking dish or line with parchment paper.

Place apples in baking dish. Set aside.

In a saucepan over medium heat, combine brown sugar, butter, and 3 tablespoons water. Cook until clear, about 5 minutes. Pour over apples.

In a bowl, sift together flour, baking soda, ginger, cloves, and salt. Set aside.

In another bowl, cream shortening and sugar until light and fluffy. Add egg and mix until well blended. Alternately add flour mixture and molasses. Add hot water and mix until smooth.

Pour over apples and bake for 50 minutes, or until a toothpick inserted into the center comes out clean.

Serve with ice cream or your favorite topping.

Makes 6 servings.

I found this recipe in Gramma's well-worn and discolored 1939 recipe book. It's got to be good, right? So I tried it and it turned out to be wonderful!

Kitty Bryan, Longview, Washington

DESSERTS: PIES & PUDDINGS

DEWBERRY COBBLER

Dewberries are like blackberries but smaller and rarer. Blackberries are a fine substitute. Blueberries would be, too. The amount of sugar used on the berries seemed like a lot for some tasters; it can be reduced without harming the outcome. Expect several volunteers to scrape the baking dish clean! –C.S.

¾ cup all-purpose flour

2 teaspoons baking powder

½ teaspoon salt

1½ cups sugar, divided

¾ cup milk

½ cup (1 stick) butter

3 cups dewberries or blackberries

Preheat oven to 350°F.

In a bowl, combine flour, baking powder, and salt. Add 1 cup of sugar and slowly pour in milk. Mix until all lumps are dissolved.

Melt butter in an 8x8-inch or similar-size baking pan. Pour batter over butter. Do not stir.

Toss dewberries with remaining ½ cup of sugar. Carefully spoon over batter. Bake for 1 hour.

Makes 8 to 10 servings.

I am now 59 years old and remember this recipe from the time I was 4 or 5. My "Aunt Willie Mae" (not my aunt, but my neighbor) made this cobbler for the annual Father's Day picnic every June. She and my mother would take us kids to pick berries when they were ripe. Every chance I had, I would request Aunt Willie Mae's cobbler because it was the very best. I have since moved across the state, and just last year, my son, who is also a dewberry lover, planted a dewberry bush in my garden. The tradition lives on!

Billye White, Fayetteville, Arkansas

To test the freshness of baking powder, add 1 teaspoon
to a cup of hot water. If the mixture bubbles a lot,
it's good; if it doesn't, throw it out.

APPLE WALNUT PEACH CRISP WITH CINNAMON BROWN SUGAR CRUMBLE

TESTER'S COMMENTS

This combination is a winner! What's more, if fresh peaches are not available, even canned, drained, work well. –C.S.

3 cups peeled, cored, and sliced Golden Delicious apples

2 cups peeled, pitted, and sliced peaches

4 tablespoons sugar

½ cup old-fashioned oats

½ cup brown sugar

¼ cup all-purpose flour

½ teaspoon ground cinnamon

¼ cup (½ stick) butter

¼ cup chopped walnuts

Preheat oven to 375°F. Grease a 2-quart baking dish.

In a bowl, toss together apples, peaches, and sugar. Pour into baking dish.

In another bowl, combine oats, brown sugar, flour, and cinnamon. Cut in butter until mixture is crumbly. Mix in walnuts. Sprinkle over fruit. Bake for 30 minutes, or until fruit is tender and topping is golden. Serve warm.

Makes 6 to 8 servings.

Living in the cold Northeast when I was younger, I learned to appreciate the value of a comforting, warm dessert that not only tasted good but also warmed your belly. This delicious crisp will do just that! My family has served crisps during the cold months for generations. (OK, yes: We served them even in the summertime.) I grew up with apple, peach, and blueberry crisp. It's delicious warm, room temperature, or cold. This one is a combination of my two favorites, apple and peach.

Angela Spengler, Tampa, Florida

Old-fashioned oats are whole rolled oats that are steamed and then flattened. Quick-cooking oats are whole rolled oats that are steamed and then chopped into small pieces.

DESSERTS: PIES & PUDDINGS

GRAPE-NUTS PUDDING

This pudding is smooth, creamy, and slightly sweet. Eat it cold, room temperature, or warm; no matter which way, it is comfort food in a bowl! –S.L.P.

4 cups milk

1 cup Grape-Nuts cereal

4 eggs

scant ½ cup sugar

2½ teaspoons vanilla extract

¼ teaspoon salt

¼ to ½ teaspoon ground nutmeg

whipped cream (optional)

Heat oven to 350°F. Butter a 2-quart baking dish.

In a saucepan over medium heat, bring milk and Grape-Nuts to a simmer. Remove from heat, stir, and let cool 15 minutes.

In a bowl, beat eggs with sugar, vanilla, and salt. Add cooled milk mixture and stir well.

Pour into prepared baking dish. Sprinkle nutmeg over pudding. Set baking dish into a deep roasting pan. Place in oven and add enough water into the roasting pan to reach halfway up the side of the dish. Bake for 50 to 60 minutes, or until almost set in the center—a toothpick inserted into the center should come out clean. Let pudding cool for at least 20 minutes before serving. Serve plain or with whipped cream.

Makes 8 servings.

Almanac favorite

To keep eggs fresh, store them in your refrigerator in their original carton.
It protects them from drying out and absorbing odors.

DESSERTS: PIES & PUDDINGS

RAISIN PUDDING

These ingredients are kitchen staples (nothing fancy here) and it goes into the oven quickly, so it's easy to make on the spur of the moment. The nutmeg flavor was one taster's favorite part. Others described it as true comfort food and a treat for any sweet tooth. –D.T.

½ cup raisins

hot water

Pudding:

1 cup all-purpose flour

1 teaspoon baking powder

½ teaspoon baking soda

¼ teaspoon ground nutmeg

¼ teaspoon salt

½ cup sugar

1 tablespoon butter, melted

½ cup milk

¼ teaspoon vanilla extract

½ cup chopped walnuts or sliced almonds
  (optional)

Sauce:

2 cups boiling water

1 cup brown sugar

2 tablespoons (¼ stick) butter

Preheat oven to 350°F. Grease a 9x5-inch loaf pan.

Cover raisins with hot water and let soak.

For pudding: In a bowl, sift together flour, baking powder, baking soda, nutmeg, and salt.

In another bowl, combine sugar and butter. Mix well. Add flour mixture, ⅓ cup at a time, alternately with milk. Add vanilla, drained raisins, and walnuts (if using) and stir to blend. Pour into prepared pan.

For sauce: In a bowl, combine boiling water, brown sugar, and butter. Whisk to blend.

Pour sauce over pudding mixture.

Bake for 40 to 45 minutes.

Makes 8 to 10 servings.

This is my dad's mother's recipe. She always made it around Thanksgiving and Christmas. It is a real comfort food for me. After Nana died at the age of 100, I couldn't find her recipe, and no one else in the family had saved it. I recently discovered it while cleaning out a kitchen cupboard. I hope you like it as much as I do.

Anonymous

❧ SWEDISH RICE PUDDING ❧

This is a traditional baked rice pudding dessert in Sweden—and easy to make. At Christmastime, a blanched almond is hidden in the pudding, which is sometimes served with milk and topped with cinnamon. Tasters liked the flavor and texture. Instead of instant rice, you can use regular white rice. Either way, it's important to cook the rice in milk for a richer flavor. –M.A.J.

1 cup instant rice

2 cups milk, plus more to cook rice

½ cup (1 stick) butter

3 eggs

½ cup sugar

1 tablespoon vanilla extract

1 teaspoon salt

½ cup raisins or more, if desired

Preheat oven to 350°F. Butter an 8x8-inch glass baking dish.

Prepare instant rice according to package directions, using milk instead of water and stirring often so that rice doesn't burn. Remove from heat and stir in butter while hot so that butter melts without lumps.

In a bowl, combine 2 cups of milk, eggs, sugar, vanilla, and salt and stir to blend. Fold in rice mixture and raisins.

Pour into prepared dish and bake for 50 minutes.

Makes 6 servings.

This recipe was passed down from my great-grandmother MiMi to my grandmother Thelma to my mother, Ann, and then to me. I have it memorized and sometimes double or triple it (mixing it in a gallon pitcher). I can eat one serving for dinner dessert and another for the next morning's breakfast. The other servings I bring to my mother, who is now in a nursing home, and to my stepfather, who visits her every day.

Kimberly George, Chicago, Illinois

DESSERTS: PIES & PUDDINGS

PERSIMMON PUDDING

This bakes into a dense cake with an almost-cookie crust around a moist center. (Lovers of cake edges and loaf ends will find the "chew" of those parts irresistible here.) Tasters were reminded of gingerbread. Several longed for whipped cream or ice cream on top—great ideas, when the pudding is warm. –L.R.

2 cups puréed persimmons (4 to 5 fruit)

2 cups self-rising flour

1½ cups sweetened condensed milk

1 cup sugar

1 cup brown sugar

1 teaspoon ground cinnamon

2 eggs

Preheat oven to 375°F. Lightly coat a 13x9-inch baking dish with nonstick cooking spray.

Mix together persimmons, flour, milk, sugars, cinnamon, and eggs.

Pour into prepared dish. Bake for 1 hour, or until a toothpick inserted into the center comes out clean. Cool for 30 minutes before serving.

Makes 8 servings.

I grew up on persimmon pudding and began to experiment. I came up with this, and everyone in my family loves it. Hope y'all enjoy it.

Keith Gunter, Advance, North Carolina

HOW TO MAKE SELF-RISING FLOUR
For every cup of all-purpose flour, add 1½ teaspoons baking powder and ½ teaspoon salt. Mix well.

KRUM KAGER

TESTER'S COMMENTS

When made properly, these cookies resemble delicate ice cream cones, but they taste sweeter and more buttery. Filled with berries and/or whipped cream, they are elegant—even regal. I borrowed a krum kage iron and cone tool from a Norwegian friend. (When I shared the recipe, she suggested using 1 teaspoon cardamom instead of vanilla.) Once the krum kage iron was hot, the cookies baked quickly and were easy to roll. It might be possible to cook them in a regular cast iron pan like crepes, but rolling them into a cone shape without a cone tool would be a challenge. –M.A.J.

3 eggs

1 cup sugar

1 cup (2 sticks) butter, melted

1 can (5 ounces) evaporated milk

1½ cups all-purpose flour

1 teaspoon vanilla extract

Preheat krum kage iron on stovetop burner over medium heat for about 10 minutes.

In a bowl, beat eggs well, add sugar, and continue beating. Add butter, milk, flour, and vanilla and blend thoroughly.

Brush both surfaces of krum kage iron with oil or butter and place a rounded tablespoon of batter on lower plate. Close iron and press handles together. Bake for about 30 seconds, flip over iron, and cook for about 30 seconds, or until light brown. Remove cookie from iron and roll onto cone form to shape. Set aside and repeat with remaining batter.

Makes about 4 dozen cookies.

This Scandinavian treat is light and tastes great! Children can help to make and shape the cookies.

Krystal Grooters, Raleigh, North Carolina

To properly make Krum Kager, you need a special krum kage [pl. "kager"] iron that sits on the stovetop, plus a special wooden cone on which to roll the cookies while they are warm.

DESSERTS: COOKIES & BARS

GREAT-GRANDMA CLARA'S CHRISTMAS SUGAR COOKIES

It's important for the dough to rest in the refrigerator before being rolled. I would suggest for 3 hours. It stays easy to work with even after more than a day of chilling. –C.S.

DESSERTS: COOKIES & BARS

Cookies:

3 eggs

1 cup sugar

1 cup (2 sticks) margarine, softened

1 teaspoon vanilla extract

2 to 3 cups all-purpose flour

1 teaspoon baking soda

½ teaspoon salt

Egg paint:

1 egg yolk

food coloring

For cookies: Separate 1 egg. Set aside white. Combine yolk with 2 eggs and beat well.

In a bowl, cream sugar and margarine. Add well-beaten eggs to creamed mixture. Add vanilla and stir to blend.

In another bowl, sift together flour, baking soda, and salt.

Add flour mixture to margarine mixture a little at a time. Beat well. Repeat until fully incorporated. (You will need enough flour to make a rollable dough. If dough is too stiff, add milk; if too soft, add flour.) Chill dough for at least 1 hour.

Preheat oven to 350°F. Line a baking sheet with parchment paper.

Working with one-quarter of dough at a time, roll it between two sheets of wax paper: Lightly flour wax paper on counter surface. Place dough in center and lightly flour. Cover with wax paper and roll to a ¼- to ⅛-inch thickness. Use cookie cutters to cut desired shapes and place on baking sheet.

Beat remaining egg white with 1 tablespoon water. Paint egg wash on cookies, decorate with egg paint (see below), if desired. Bake for 6 to 10 minutes, or until lightly browned and firm to the touch. Cool for 5 minutes, then transfer to a cooling rack.

For egg paint: In a bowl, stir together egg yolk and a small amount of food coloring. Add more to achieve desired color.

Using a small paintbrush, decorate unbaked cookies with egg paint, freehand or with a stencil. Bake as directed.

Makes 50 to 60 cookies, depending on size.

When my paternal grandma died at age 82, no one wanted her massive recipe collection, so I took it. I found this 3x5-inch index card with my great-grandma's name on it with only a list of ingredients. I had to fix it and finish it based on what I knew about making cookies. I still give Great-Grandma credit for the recipe, and it is now a tradition. Every year for Christmas, I make these cookies as gifts for friends and family. They are always a hit! Thank you, Great-Grandma Clara!

Carol Glynn, Hawk Point, Missouri

❧ SESAME CRISPS ❧

TESTER'S COMMENTS

Since testing this recipe, I've made it over and over. The cookies bake thin and crisp. Serve them with fruit sorbets or almost any flavor of ice cream. –C.S.

½ cup all-purpose flour

⅛ teaspoon salt

⅛ teaspoon baking soda

1 cup packed brown sugar

½ cup (1 stick) unsalted butter, softened

1 egg

½ cup sesame seeds

Adjust rack to lower third of oven. Preheat oven to 325°F. Line a baking sheet with parchment paper.

In a bowl, sift together flour, salt, and baking soda.

In another bowl, cream brown sugar and butter. Add egg and blend well. Stir in flour mixture and sesame seeds.

Drop batter by rounded ½ teaspoonfuls about 2 inches apart onto prepared baking sheet. Bake for 6 to 8 minutes. Cookies will puff up, then flatten and brown.

Set baking sheet on a cooling rack. Cool completely before removing.

Makes about 4½ dozen cookies.

Almanac favorite

Sesame seeds come in a variety of colors, including white, yellow, red, and black.

❧ GINGER CREAMS ❧

These cookies have a cakelike texture and taste like really good, dark gingerbread (so dark that they might be mistaken for chocolate). The frosting helps to offset their intensity—that is, if you think they're intense. I frosted the flat bottoms of two dozen cookies and topped them with the remaining cookies, making "sandwiches," which made them doubly sweet treats. –D.T.

Cookies:

⅓ cup shortening

½ cup sugar

½ cup molasses

1 egg, beaten

2 cups all-purpose flour

1 teaspoon ground ginger

½ teaspoon ground cinnamon

½ teaspoon ground nutmeg

½ teaspoon salt

½ teaspoon baking soda

Frosting:

2 cups confectioners' sugar

¼ cup (½ stick) butter, softened

1 teaspoon vanilla extract

1 tablespoon milk, plus more if needed

For cookies: In a bowl, combine shortening, sugar, molasses, and egg. Add ½ cup water and stir to blend.

In another bowl, mix together flour, ginger, cinnamon, nutmeg, salt, and baking soda. Add to molasses mixture, stir to blend, and refrigerate for 1 hour.

Preheat oven to 375°F.

Drop by teaspoonfuls about 2 inches apart onto a baking sheet. Bake for 8 to 10 minutes, or until cookies spring back when touched. Transfer to a cooling rack.

For frosting: In a bowl, combine sugar and butter. Add vanilla and stir. Add milk and stir, adding more milk until frosting is easy to spread. Frost cookies.

Makes 4 dozen cookies.

My mother always made these. They were quick to make. I still make them but never think they are as good as hers.
Diana Severson, Monroe, Wisconsin

❧ BUTTERY GINGERSNAPS ❧

1 cup sugar, plus more for coating

¾ cup butter (1½ sticks), melted or very soft, plus more for flattening

¼ cup molasses or dark corn syrup

1 egg

2 cups all-purpose flour

2 teaspoons baking soda

1 teaspoon ground cinnamon

1 teaspoon ground ginger

½ teaspoon ground cloves

½ teaspoon salt

In a bowl, cream sugar and butter. Add molasses and egg and mix well.

In another bowl, sift together flour, baking soda, cinnamon, ginger, cloves, and salt and add to butter mixture. Mix well, cover tightly, and refrigerate. (Batter is easier to shape when well chilled, several hours or overnight.)

Preheat oven to 375°F. Grease a baking sheet.

Put some sugar into a shallow bowl. Form batter into 1-inch balls. Roll each ball in sugar. Place on prepared baking sheet about 2 inches apart.

Butter the bottom of a drinking glass or jelly jar and dip in sugar. Flatten each ball using the glass or jar. Bake for 8 to 10 minutes, or until golden brown. Cool for 1 to 2 minutes, then remove to a cooling rack.

Makes 3 dozen cookies.

These cookies have been a perennial holiday favorite. Use butter, not margarine, for best results. Make the dough ahead and then make cookies as you wish. The flavor is even better when several days old.

Anonymous

Allow baking sheets to cool completely before filling with another batch of cookies.

GLUTEN-FREE CHOCOLATE–COCONUT–CRANBERRY COOKIES

Everyone swooned for these. They have an airy, almost meringue-like texture, yet lots of chew, thanks to the oats and coconut. The cranberries and chocolate "pop" with flavor. –C.S.

1 cup unsalted almond butter

½ cup sugar (or a little less, if you prefer)

1 egg

½ teaspoon vanilla extract

dash of ground cinnamon

1 bar (1.75 ounces) dark chocolate, chopped

½ cup old-fashioned oats

½ cup dried cranberries

½ cup unsweetened or sweetened coconut flakes

Preheat oven to 350°F.

In a bowl, combine almond butter, sugar, egg, vanilla, and cinnamon and mix well. Add chocolate, oats, cranberries, and coconut.

Drop by rounded tablespoons onto a baking sheet. Bake for 10 to 13 minutes. Cool for at least 5 minutes on baking sheet to avoid crumbled cookies.

Makes 12 to 18 cookies.

My daughter was born with severe intolerance to soy, dairy, wheat, and corn. When she was older, I felt bad that she couldn't eat a lot of things that other kids her age could eat, so I created this recipe for her.

Jenna Luv, Concord, California

You can substitute peanut butter for almond butter; if you
have a nut allergy, substitute sunflower butter.

❦ TYE'S FAVORITE CHOCOLATE DROP COOKIES ❦

An easy and delicious cookie! Soft, the way I like it. –L.R.

1 cup sugar

½ cup (1 stick) butter, softened

1 egg

¾ cup milk

2 cups sifted all-purpose flour

2 teaspoons baking powder

2 squares (1 ounce each) unsweetened baking chocolate

½ teaspoon vanilla extract

Preheat oven to 425°F. Grease a baking sheet.

In a bowl, cream sugar and butter until smooth.

In another bowl, beat egg and stir in milk. Add slowly to butter mixture and beat together with wooden spoon.

In a separate bowl, sift together flour and baking powder. Add to butter mixture and beat with spoon.

In a double boiler over boiling water, melt chocolate squares. Add to batter. Add vanilla and stir to blend well.

Drop by teaspoonfuls about 2 inches apart onto prepared baking sheet. Bake for 7 to 10 minutes. Remove from oven as soon as they are done so that they stay soft.

Makes 12 to 18 cookies.

My mother dealt with serious mental illness, and there were few good memories in the generations of our family relating to her interactions. A wonderful one was her love of recipes. Not of cooking or baking, but of recipes. She would read a cookbook like a piece of fiction and then write down her ideas that came from the thousands of recipes and her envisioning of what would be good. One Christmas, she offered me this recipe and I made them, only to find that our youngest nephew, who lived with us, declared them to be his favorite chocolate drop cookies ever. It still is, even now that he is in his 30s!

Doe West, Sturbridge, Massachusetts

ℰ CREAM OF COCONUT MACAROON COOKIES ℘

TESTER'S COMMENTS

Tasters loved the true macaroon chew and taste. A few thought that these were a little too sweet; using unsweetened coconut flakes and eliminating the extract would make them less so. The remaining ingredients have plenty of coconut flavor. While this recipe is easy to make (no egg whites to whip, as with other macaroon recipes), the ingredients can be hard to find. Look for meringue powder at craft stores or natural food stores. Coconut flour can be found in stores and online. –M.A.J.

1 can (15 ounces) cream of coconut

2 teaspoons meringue powder

1 teaspoon coconut extract

1 tablespoon hot water

1 package sweetened coconut flakes

⅔ cups coconut flour

Preheat oven to 350°F. Line two baking sheets with parchment paper.

In a bowl, combine cream of coconut, meringue powder, coconut extract, and hot water. Stir until combined. Fold in coconut flakes and flour.

Drop by rounded tablespoons onto prepared baking sheets. For broader cookies, dip your fingers into a bowl of warm water and lightly press down each cookie (do not flatten).

Bake, one sheet at a time, for 15 to 20 minutes, or until edges are golden. Rotate sheet 180 degrees halfway through baking. Slide parchment paper, with cookies, off baking sheet and onto cooling racks.

Makes about 2 to 3 dozen cookies, depending on size.

I love to challenge myself when making cookies for my family and friends. I make these cookies for Christmas. I add a few drops of red food coloring to half of the mixture and a few drops of green food coloring to the other half just to be festive for the holidays. My husband, family, and friends love them.

Karen Payette, Lyndonville, Vermont

❧ BLUEBERRY WALNUT OATMEAL COOKIES ❧

TESTER'S COMMENTS

These have nice chunk and chew and are pleasingly light. It's well worth finding soy flour and maple sugar (be aware that maple sugar is pricey). Do not try to substitute maple syrup or brown sugar. –J.S.

1¼ cups maple sugar

¾ cup shortening or light butter

¼ cup milk

3 tablespoons honey

2 teaspoons vanilla extract

1 extra-large egg

3 cups uncooked quick-cooking oats

1 cup soy flour

1 teaspoon ground cinnamon

½ teaspoon baking soda

1 cup blueberries

1 cup chopped walnuts

Preheat oven to 350°F. Line a baking sheet with parchment paper.

In a bowl, combine maple sugar, shortening, milk, honey, vanilla, and egg and beat until creamy.

In another bowl, combine oats, flour, cinnamon, and baking soda. Add to egg mixture by hand or beat on low speed until incorporated. Mix in blueberries and walnuts by hand. Drop by heaping tablespoons at least 1 inch apart onto prepared baking sheet. Bake for 12 minutes or until lightly browned. Cool for a few minutes, then transfer to a cooling rack.

Makes 2 dozen cookies.

I came up with this recipe for a heart healthy cookie for my husband, who loves cookies.
Melia Koerner, New Carlisle, Ohio

Bake only one sheet of cookies at a time, on the center rack.
This allows for the most even baking.

DESSERTS: COOKIES & BARS

❧ Mom's Forgotten Mint Cookies ❧

These cookies took very little effort to produce a light, crisp, and refreshing result. –S.L.P.

2 egg whites, at room temperature

¾ cup sugar

½ cup mini chocolate chips

¼ teaspoon mint extract

1 to 2 drops green food coloring

Preheat oven to 375°F. Line a baking sheet with parchment paper.

In a bowl, beat egg whites until stiff, gradually adding sugar. Fold in chocolate chips, mint extract, and food coloring.

Drop by teaspoonfuls on prepared baking sheet.

Place in oven and turn off immediately. Leave in oven with door closed overnight.

Makes about 3 dozen small cookies.

Almanac favorite

VARIATIONS

Try experimenting with different extracts and food colorings to make numerous treats: orange extract with red and yellow coloring, cherry extract with red coloring, lemon extract with yellow coloring, and coconut extract without any coloring.

PEG'S BLACK BEAN BROWNIES

TESTER'S COMMENTS

Tasters were surprised to learn that these brownies contained black beans. The rich and fudgy taste was enough to convince me that these brownies deserve a spot in my recipe box. –S.L.P.

1 can (15 ounces) black beans, drained and rinsed, or 2 cups cooked

3 eggs

¾ cup sugar

¼ cup unsweetened cocoa powder

3 tablespoons vegetable oil, or 1½ tablespoons olive oil plus 1½ tablespoons butter

½ teaspoon baking powder

pinch of salt

½ cup dark chocolate chips

½ cup chopped walnuts

Preheat oven to 350°F. Grease an 8x8-inch baking dish.

Combine beans, eggs, sugar, cocoa, oil, baking powder, and salt in blender or food processor and blend until smooth. Transfer to a bowl. Stir in chocolate chips and walnuts. Pour into prepared baking dish. Bake for 35 minutes, or until a toothpick inserted into the center comes out clean.

Makes 16 brownies.

Black beans add about 24 grams of protein and 20 grams of fiber to a conventional brownie recipe—and nobody will know!
Margaret Boyles, Salisbury, New Hampshire

According to food lore, the chocolate brownie was
discovered by accident in the early 1900s when someone baked
a chocolate cake and forgot to add baking powder.

DESSERTS: COOKIES & BARS

❧ OATMEAL BERRY BARS ❧

TESTER'S COMMENTS

These bars came together quickly one weekday morning. At work, tasters had one with coffee. Another after lunch. And, if the empty dish was a clue, another at home that evening. (I think they liked them!) I used a 12.5-ounce jar of sugar-free seedless raspberry preserves and it was plenty, although we should all try every fruit under the Sun. For a bit more chew, substitute almond meal for half of the flour and add toasted, chopped nuts to the batter. –J.S.

2 cups all-purpose flour

2 cups old-fashioned oats

1 cup sugar

1 teaspoon baking soda

¼ teaspoon salt

¾ cup (1½ sticks) margarine, melted

2 teaspoons vanilla extract

1 jar (10 to 16 ounces) raspberry, cherry, or strawberry jam

Preheat oven to 350°F. Grease a 13x9-inch baking dish.

In a bowl, combine flour, oats, sugar, baking soda, and salt. Add margarine and vanilla and mix until crumbly. Reserve half of mixture.

Press remaining mixture into bottom of prepared baking dish. Spread jam evenly on top of this layer. Sprinkle reserved crumbly mixture evenly on top. Bake for 20 to 25 minutes, or until lightly browned.

Makes 18 to 24 bars.

I grew raspberries for years at our former home. My children were little and loved fresh raspberries, but most years we had an overabundance. I began making raspberry jam. Lots of raspberry jam. So I looked for ways to use my jam, and these bars became an instant hit. Well, my children are grown now, but this recipe is still a popular request. Most recently I used a jar of cherry preserves that were a delicious alternative.

Julie Costello, Muncie, Indiana

After baking, refrigerate bars for a couple of hours before slicing. Chilling firms the bars and results in cleaner cuts.

Momma's Salted Shortbread Caramel Bars

TESTER'S COMMENTS

This is very, very rich, with lots of butter and cream. I made it and brought it to a church luncheon, and everyone had the same reaction: scrumptious, but very rich! A sliver is plenty for most people. –L.R.

Shortbread:

2 cups (4 sticks) butter, softened

1½ cups confectioners' sugar

1 cup sugar

2 tablespoons vanilla extract

4 cups sifted all-purpose flour

Caramel:

2 cups sugar

¾ cup (1½ sticks) butter

1 cup heavy or whipping cream

1 teaspoon sea salt, plus more for sprinkling

Preheat oven to 350°. Butter a 13x9-inch baking dish.

For shortbread: In a bowl, whip butter. Add sugars and mix well. Add vanilla and mix until incorporated. Add flour, 1 cup at a time, and mix until a soft ball forms. Put half of dough in refrigerator, covered. Press remaining dough into bottom and halfway up sides of prepared baking pan. Prick dough with fork. Bake for 20 to 25 minutes, or until edges are just slightly golden. Reduce oven to 325°F.

For caramel: Place sugar in a saucepan over low heat and stir every few minutes, until melted and caramel-color. Add butter and stir gently with wooden spoon until melted. Increase heat to just under medium and cook, stirring, until butter is just incorporated. Add cream slowly and turn off heat. Stir until fully blended. Add sea salt. Stir. Set aside for 10 minutes. Reserve ½ cup caramel sauce.

To assemble: Pour remainder of caramel onto baked shortbread. Sprinkle lightly with salt. Remove dough from refrigerator and crumble over salt and caramel. Drizzle reserved caramel sauce on top and sprinkle lightly with salt. Bake for 25 to 30 minutes, or until slightly golden. Remove from oven and cool before serving (if your family will let you).

Makes 3 dozen bars.

We (my grandma and I) were making caramels and I messed up the recipe, so we ended up with caramel sauce instead. My grandma said, No worries, I have the perfect thing for that—and showed me how to make shortbread dough. I think she must have made it many times before because she whipped it together like it was a batch of biscuits. (You would have to know my grandma and her story, but because she had 12 children, she knew how to cook.) That's how I learned to make caramel shortbread bars. Thank you, Grandma.

Amy Neiter, Mauckport, Indiana

❧ TREASURE CHEST BARS ❧

TESTER'S COMMENTS

Hide this treasure—these bars are dangerously good. None of the tasters could eat just one, no matter what the wager. I used dried apricots but want to make them with every dried fruit . . . and then with combinations of fruits. –D.T.

Bars:

½ cup (1 stick) unsalted butter, softened

⅔ cup packed brown sugar

¼ cup sugar

2 eggs

1 teaspoon vanilla extract

2 cups all-purpose flour

½ teaspoon baking powder

½ teaspoon salt

¾ cup milk

1 cup semisweet chocolate chips

¾ cup chopped pecans

½ cup chopped dried cherries, apricots, cranberries, or fruit of your choice

Frosting:

¼ cup (½ stick) unsalted butter

2 cups confectioners' sugar

2 tablespoons milk

½ teaspoon vanilla extract

pinch of salt

For bars: Adjust rack to middle of oven. Preheat oven to 350°F. Line a 13x9-inch baking dish with aluminum foil, draping it over sides (to make the bars easier to remove). Grease foil with butter.

In a bowl, combine butter, brown sugar, and sugar and beat for 2 minutes, or until creamed. Add eggs and vanilla and beat for 1 minute more.

In another bowl, whisk together flour, baking powder, and salt. Add to butter mixture in three batches, alternating with milk. Add chocolate chips, nuts, and fruit and stir to combine.

Spread batter in prepared dish. Bake for 30 minutes (rotating pan 180 degrees halfway through baking), or until the top is golden brown or a toothpick inserted into the center comes out clean. Cool bars in pan for 10 minutes. Lift foil to remove from pan.

For frosting: Melt butter in a skillet over medium-low heat, stirring, until it begins to brown. Transfer to a bowl. Add confectioners' sugar, milk, vanilla, and salt. Beat until smooth. Frost bars while still slightly warm.

Makes about 20 bars.

These bars, a variation on a fruitcake, were popular in the 1960s and '70s. This recipe came from Armand Riendeau, a soft-spoken French-Canadian chef who operated the Pot Luck Restaurant in Berlin, New Hampshire, from 1964 until 1981. Armand's son, Roland, an executive chef, said of the bars: "They had a browned-butter frosting, and that's really different."

Almanac favorite

♔ BAKED APPLE SQUARES ♕

TESTER'S COMMENTS

While this recipe comes together quickly and easily at any time of year, it's a must-make in the fall, especially after apple picking. The bars are moist inside and lightly caramelized outside. Any apple variety is suitable, but tart may be best. —D.T.

1¾ cups sugar

3 eggs

2 cups sifted all-purpose flour

1 teaspoon baking powder

1 teaspoon ground cinnamon

½ teaspoon salt

1 cup vegetable oil

1 teaspoon vanilla extract

2 cups peeled, cored, and chopped apples
(about 2 apples)

Preheat oven to 350°F. Grease a 13x9-inch baking dish.

In a bowl, combine sugar and eggs and beat until light in color. Add flour, baking powder, cinnamon, and salt and stir to blend. Add oil and vanilla and stir. Fold in apples.

Pour into prepared baking dish. Bake for 35 to 40 minutes. Transfer to a cooling rack. Cut into squares.

Makes 2 dozen squares.

I used to be a member of the local Grange, and one year we had an apple squares baking contest. This was the recipe provided to all contestants to use. My first baking contest, and I won! Every fall, I bake these apple squares and tell my family stories of my involvement in the Grange.

Holly Densmore, Buxton, Maine

Fuji, Granny Smith, and Winesap are excellent
varieties of apples to use for baking.

❧ ÉCLAIRS ❧

This was my most successful attempt ever at making éclairs, and so worth it. The puffs came out hollow (perfect for filling with cream), the filling luscious and thick (give in to licking the pan!), and the chocolate topping divine. Want to impress someone? This is a sure thing. –D.T.

DESSERTS: TOO GOOD TO LEAVE OUT

Puffs:

½ cup (1 stick) butter

1 cup all-purpose flour

4 eggs

Filling:

½ cup sugar

⅓ cup all-purpose flour

½ teaspoon salt

2 eggs

2 cups whole milk

2 teaspoons vanilla extract

Topping:

1 ounce unsweetened baking chocolate

1 teaspoon butter

2 tablespoons hot water

1 cup confectioners' sugar

Preheat oven to 400°F. Line a baking sheet with parchment paper.

For puffs: In a saucepan, heat butter and 1 cup water to a boil. Add flour and stir vigorously over low heat, until mixture forms a ball. Remove from heat. Beat in eggs all at once and continue beating until smooth. Drop dough in balls onto prepared baking sheet. Bake for 35 to 40 minutes, or until puffy and golden brown. Cool.

For filling: In a bowl, combine sugar, flour, and salt.

In another bowl, beat eggs. Add to flour mixture and stir until well combined.

In a saucepan, heat milk to almost boiling (until milk forms bubbles at edge of pan.) Add milk, a small ladleful at a time, to flour mixture and whisk vigorously. Repeat, using about half of milk. Combine flour mixture and remaining milk in saucepan and whisk to blend. Bring to a boil, stirring constantly. When mixture is thick, like pudding, it should also be just starting to boil. Remove from heat. Add vanilla and whisk to blend. Let cool.

Slice cooled puffs (horizontally or vertically) and add filling.

For topping: In a saucepan, melt chocolate and butter over low heat. Remove from heat and stir in hot water. Mix until smooth. Add confectioners' sugar and mix until smooth. Drizzle over filled éclairs. Refrigerate.

Makes 8 large éclairs or 36 mini éclairs.

This was my Danish grandmother's recipe. My mother made it for us often while we were growing up. It is a family favorite and requested often.

Lynne Kuhne, Sonora, California

❦ PHIL'S CHOCOLATE SAUCE ❧

For best results, follow this recipe exactly as written. Ice cream and/or cake are optional. You could just as easily enjoy it with only a spoon. –J.S.

4 ounces semisweet chocolate squares
  (not chips)
½ cup (1 stick) butter
1 cup sugar
½ cup milk
dash of salt (optional)
dash of vanilla extract (optional)

Melt together chocolate and butter in saucepan. Add sugar, milk, and salt and vanilla (if using). Stir until mixture starts to boil. Boil for precisely 2½ minutes, then remove from heat. Set aside for 30 minutes, stirring occasionally. Pour over ice cream.

Makes about 3 cups.

I grew up watching my parents make everything from scratch. Almost all of the meals and treats that they made have been passed down from generation to generation. One of my favorite things was my stepdad's chocolate sauce. It is so easy to make and so delicious to eat, you will never again bother with store-bought chocolate sauce!

Kirsten O'Connell, Dublin, New Hampshire

Around 1517, Spanish explorer Hernando Cortés
tasted cacao, liked it, and called it "chocolat" because he
had difficulty in pronouncing its Aztec name, *xocolatl.*

CHOCOLATE MONKEY TRUFFLES

TESTER'S COMMENTS

All treats should be this quick, easy, and "healthy"-tasting! I used smooth peanut butter but will try crunchy next time, and I'll add granola or oats—why not? Loved them! –M.S.

1 jar (18 ounces) peanut butter
2½ cups confectioners' sugar
¼ cup (½ stick) butter
2 teaspoons vanilla extract
2 large ripe bananas
1 bag (23 ounces) milk chocolate chips

In a bowl, microwave peanut butter for a few seconds. If it gets too warm and becomes runny, refrigerate it for about 20 minutes before proceeding.

Add confectioners' sugar, butter, and vanilla to peanut butter. Stir until blended.

Mash bananas with a fork. Fold into peanut butter mixture. Shape batter into 1-inch balls. Place on a baking sheet. Transfer to freezer for about 20 minutes to firm.

Melt chocolate chips according to package directions.

One at a time, stick a toothpick into each ball, dip into melted chocolate, and allow excess to drip off. Return ball to baking sheet to dry. Repeat for each ball. Store in a storage bag in refrigerator or freezer.

Makes 10 to 12 servings, depending on size.

My husband covers bananas with chocolate all the time and sticks them in the freezer, and I make protein balls with peanut butter all the time, so I decided to combine the two.

Laura Smith, Harrisburg, Missouri

If you find yourself without confectioners' sugar, simply place granulated sugar in a blender or food processor and pulse several times.

TOFFEE POPCORN

This sinfully delicious snack is just too easy. My family and I ate it until the bowl was bare, dreaming of ways to make it even better, like adding roasted peanuts in place of, or in addition to, toffee bits, turning it into something kind of like the snack in a little box with a prize inside. –S.L.P.

12 cups popped popcorn (½ cup unpopped kernels)
½ cup (1 stick) butter
¾ cup packed brown sugar
¼ cup honey
pinch of salt
1 teaspoon vanilla extract
⅓ cup toffee bits

Remove and discard any unpopped kernels from popcorn.

In a saucepan over medium heat, combine butter, brown sugar, honey, and salt, stirring constantly. Bring to a simmer, whisk in vanilla, and simmer for 4 to 5 minutes. The longer it cooks, the crunchier the coating will be.

Put popcorn into a bowl. Pour sauce over popcorn. Gently toss until popcorn is evenly coated. Sprinkle with toffee bits and stir until evenly incorporated.

Store in an airtight container.

Makes 12 cups.

As a family, we love popcorn. We decided to experiment one day, and voilà!—*Toffee Popcorn.*
Cary Harrington, Cypress, California

Popcorn is a whole grain and contains a good amount of dietary fiber.

❧ PEANUT BUTTER FUDGE ❧

Yummy! This is creamy fudge that comes together easily. The peanuts add a nice crunch. –C.S.

4 cups sugar

1 cup evaporated milk

½ cup (1 stick) butter

1 tablespoon white vinegar

1 tablespoon light corn syrup

1 jar (18 ounces) peanut butter

1 jar (7 ounces) marshmallow cream

1 cup peanuts, rough chopped

Butter a 13x9-inch dish.

In a saucepan, heat sugar, milk, butter, vinegar, and corn syrup to soft-ball stage on candy thermometer. Remove from heat. Add peanut butter and marshmallow cream. Stir to blend, then stir in chopped peanuts. Pour into prepared dish.

Cool completely, then cut into squares. This fudge freezes well.

Makes about 48 pieces.

My dad is 89 years old and a retired Methodist minister. His favorite dessert is peanut butter candy. While he was serving the Greenville, Virginia, church, a lady made this fudge for him. It's the best I've ever tried, and I've tried plenty. I have been making it for Christmas for him since then. The recipe is so popular that I have actually given a small class to some of the young women in our family on making this fudge. I start getting requests in October—no one wants to be left out when fudge season starts. The teachers at the local school make sure that my grandkids bring them some; even the ones who don't teach the grandkids are sending requests. I can't take the credit for the recipe, which I've tweaked to suit my taste. Elaine Shiflett is the lady to thank for the original.

Claudette Wilcher, Craigsville, Virginia

Evaporated milk has about 60% of its water content removed.
Do not confuse it with condensed milk, which is sweetened.

✒ FUDGE ICE CREAM ✒

TESTER'S COMMENTS

The thought of making homemade ice cream may seem daunting, but with this recipe, it's quite simple. This ice cream's smooth and creamy consistency had my family and I hooked! Then I gave it to the tasters . . . and nobody gave it back! –S.L.P.

½ cup evaporated cane juice crystals (raw sugar)

¼ cup granulated stevia sweetener

1 envelope unflavored gelatin

dash of salt

1 can (13.5 ounces) full-fat coconut milk

1 egg, beaten

3 ounces dark chocolate
(65%+ cacao preferred), chopped

1⅓ cups milk

1 cup whipping cream

2 teaspoons vanilla extract

In a saucepan, combine cane juice crystals, stevia, gelatin, and salt. Stir in coconut milk. Cook, stirring, over medium heat until sweetener dissolves. Do not boil.

In a bowl, stir 1 cup hot mixture into beaten egg. Return egg mixture to saucepan. Add chocolate. Cook and stir for 2 minutes more. Cool. Add milk, cream, and vanilla and stir. Transfer to an ice cream freezer and follow manufacturer's directions.

Makes 1½ quarts ice cream.

We usually do not eat processed sugar or cow's milk, but we love ice cream. We have tried making homemade ice cream several times with our goat's milk, but the texture was never quite right. After a few experiments, we came up with this recipe, and it is a keeper! The flavor is just like a Fudgsicle and the texture is divine!

Leslie Brush, Hamilton, Montana

When making ice cream, do not fill the canister more than
three-quarters full—somewhere between two-thirds and three-quarters is ideal.
If the canister gets overcrowded, your ice cream will become grainy.

Fudge Ice Cream,
Phil's Chocolate
Sauce (page 258),
and Toffee Popcorn
(page 260)

❦ SUBSTITUTIONS FOR COMMON INGREDIENTS ❧

ITEM	QUANTITY	SUBSTITUTION
Baking powder	1 teaspoon	¼ teaspoon baking soda plus ¼ teaspoon cornstarch plus ½ teaspoon cream of tartar
Buttermilk	1 cup	1 tablespoon lemon juice or white vinegar plus milk to equal 1 cup; or 1 cup plain yogurt
Chocolate, unsweetened	1 ounce	3 tablespoons cocoa plus 1 tablespoon butter, shortening, or vegetable oil (dissolve the cocoa in the recipe's liquid)
Cracker crumbs	¾ cup	1 cup dry bread crumbs; or 1 tablespoon quick-cooking oats (for thickening)
Cream, heavy	1 cup	¾ cup milk plus ⅓ cup melted butter (this will not whip)
Cream, light	1 cup	⅞ cup milk plus 3 tablespoons melted, unsalted butter
Cream, sour	1 cup	⅞ cup buttermilk or plain yogurt plus 3 tablespoons melted, unsalted butter
Cream, whipping	1 cup	⅔ cup well-chilled evaporated milk, whipped; or 1 cup nonfat dry milk powder whipped with 1 cup ice water
Egg	1 whole	2 yolks plus 1 tablespoon cold water; or 3 tablespoons vegetable oil plus 1 tablespoon water (for baking); or 2 to 3 tablespoons mayonnaise (for cakes)
Egg white	1 white	2 teaspoons meringue powder plus 3 tablespoons water, combined
Flour, all-purpose	1 cup	1 cup plus 3 tablespoons cake flour (not advised for cookies or quick breads); or 1 cup self-rising flour (omit baking powder and salt from recipe); or 1¼ cups rye or coarsely ground whole grain flour; or 1 cup cornmeal
Flour, cake	1 cup	1 cup minus 3 tablespoons sifted all-purpose flour plus 3 tablespoons cornstarch
Flour, self-rising	1 cup	1 cup all-purpose flour plus 1½ teaspoons baking powder plus ½ teaspoon salt
Herbs, dried	1 teaspoon	1 tablespoon fresh herbs, minced and packed
Honey	1 cup	1¼ cups sugar plus ½ cup liquid called for in recipe (such as water or oil)
Ketchup	1 cup	1 cup tomato sauce plus ¼ cup sugar plus 3 tablespoons apple-cider vinegar plus ½ teaspoon salt plus pinch of ground cloves combined; or 1 cup chili sauce
Lemon juice	1 teaspoon	½ teaspoon white vinegar
Mayonnaise	1 cup	1 cup sour cream or plain yogurt; or 1 cup cottage cheese (puréed)
Milk, skim	1 cup	⅓ cup instant nonfat dry milk plus ¾ cup water
Milk, sweetened condensed	1 can (14 oz.)	1 cup evaporated milk plus 1¼ cups granulated sugar. Combine and heat until sugar dissolves.
Milk, whole	1 cup	½ cup evaporated whole milk plus ½ cup water; or ¾ cup 2 percent milk plus ¼ cup half-and-half
Molasses	1 cup	1 cup honey or dark corn syrup
Mustard, dry	1 teaspoon	1 tablespoon prepared mustard less 1 teaspoon liquid from recipe
Oat bran	1 cup	1 cup wheat bran or rice bran or wheat germ
Oats, old-fashioned (rolled)	1 cup	1 cup steel-cut Irish or Scotch oats
Sugar, dark-brown	1 cup	1 cup light-brown sugar, packed; or 1 cup granulated sugar plus 2 to 3 tablespoons molasses
Sugar, granulated	1 cup	1 cup firmly packed brown sugar; or ¾ cups confectioners' sugar (makes baked goods less crisp); or 1 cup superfine sugar

REFERENCE

ITEM	QUANTITY	SUBSTITUTION
Sugar, light-brown	1 cup	1 cup granulated sugar plus 1 to 2 tablespoons molasses; or ½ cup dark-brown sugar plus ½ cup sugar
Vinegar, apple-cider	—	malt, white-wine, or rice vinegar
Vinegar, balsamic	1 tablespoon	1 tablespoon red- or white-wine vinegar plus ½ teaspoon sugar
Vinegar, red-wine	—	white-wine, sherry, champagne, or balsamic vinegar
Vinegar, rice	—	apple-cider, champagne, or white-wine vinegar
Vinegar, white-wine	—	apple-cider, champagne, fruit (raspberry), rice, or red-wine vinegar
Yeast	1 cake	1 package or 1 scant tablespoon active dried yeast
Yogurt, plain	1 cup	1 cup sour cream (thicker; less tart) or buttermilk (thinner; use in baking, dressings, sauces)

❧ Pan Sizes and Equivalents ❧

One pan size can be substituted for another, but the cooking time may change. For example, if a recipe calls for using an 8-inch round cake pan and baking for 25 minutes, and a 9-inch pan is used, the cake may bake in only 20 minutes because the batter forms a thinner layer in the larger pan.

Also, specialty pans such as tube and Bundt pans distribute heat differently. Results may vary if a regular cake pan is substituted for a specialty one, even if the volume is the same. Here's a plan for those times when the correct-size pan is unavailable:

PAN SIZE	VOLUME	PAN SUBSTITUTE
9x1¼-inch pie pan	4 cups	8x1½-inch round cake pan
8½x4½x2½-inch loaf pan	6 cups	Four 5x2¼x2-inch loaf pans or a 11x7x2-inch cake pan
9x5x3-inch loaf pan	8 cups	8x8x2-inch cake pan or a 9x2-inch round cake pan
15½x10½x1-inch jelly-roll pan	10 cups	9x9x2-inch cake pan or two 8x2-inch round cake pans or a 9x2½-inch springform pan
10x3½-inch Bundt pan	12 cups	Two 8½x4½x2½-inch loaf pans or a 9x3-inch tube pan or a 9x3-inch springform pan
13x9x2-inch cake pan	14 to 15 cups	Two 9x2-inch round cake pans or two 8x8x2-inch cake pans

If the correct-size casserole is unavailable, substitute a baking pan. Again, think about the depth of the ingredients in the dish and lengthen or shorten the baking time accordingly.

CASSEROLE SIZE	VOLUME	PAN SUBSTITUTE
1½ quarts	6 cups	8½x4½x2½-inch loaf pan
2 quarts	8 cups	8x8x2-inch cake pan
2½ quarts	10 cups	9x9x2-inch cake pan
3 quarts	12 cups	13x9x2-inch cake pan
4 quarts	16 cups	14x10x2-inch cake pan

WEIGHTS, MEASURES, AND EQUIVALENTS

COMMON HOUSEHOLD MEASURES

3 teaspoons = 1 tablespoon

16 tablespoons = 1 cup

1 cup = 8 ounces

2 cups = 1 pint

2 pints = 1 quart

4 quarts = 1 gallon

METRIC CONVERSIONS

½ teaspoon = 2 mL

1 teaspoon = 5 mL

1 tablespoon = 15 mL

¼ cup = 60 mL

⅓ cup = 75 mL

½ cup = 125 mL

⅔ cup = 150 mL

¾ cup = 175 mL

1 cup = 250 mL

1 liter = 1.057 U.S. liquid quarts

1 U.S. liquid quart = 0.946 liter

1 U.S. liquid gallon = 3.78 liters

1 gram = 0.035 ounce

1 ounce = 28.349 grams

1 kilogram = 2.2 pounds

1 pound = 0.45 kilogram

TEMPERATURE CONVERSION

To convert Fahrenheit to Celsius, subtract 32 from the Fahrenheit number, multiply by 5, and divide by 9.

VEGETABLE EQUIVALENTS

ASPARAGUS: 1 pound = 3 cups chopped

BEANS (STRING): 1 pound = 4 cups chopped

BEETS: 1 pound (5 medium) = 2½ cups chopped

BROCCOLI: ½ pound = 6 cups chopped

CABBAGE: 1 pound = 4½ cups shredded

CARROTS: 1 pound = 3½ cups sliced or grated

CELERY: 1 pound = 4 cups chopped

CUCUMBERS: 1 pound (2 medium) = 4 cups sliced

EGGPLANT: 1 pound = 4 cups chopped = 2 cups cooked

GARLIC: 1 clove = 1 teaspoon chopped

LEEKS: 1 pound = 4 cups chopped = 2 cups cooked

MUSHROOMS: 1 pound = 5 to 6 cups sliced = 2 cups cooked

ONIONS: 1 pound = 4 cups sliced = 2 cups cooked

PARSNIPS: 1 pound unpeeled = 1½ cups cooked, puréed

PEAS: 1 pound whole = 1 to 1½ cups shelled

POTATOES: 1 pound (3 medium) sliced = 2 cups mashed

PUMPKIN: 1 pound = 4 cups chopped = 2 cups cooked and drained

SPINACH: 1 pound = ¾ to 1 cup cooked

SQUASHES (SUMMER): 1 pound = 4 cups grated = 2 cups sliced and cooked

SQUASHES (WINTER): 2 pounds = 2½ cups cooked, puréed

SWEET POTATOES: 1 pound = 4 cups grated = 1 cup cooked, puréed

SWISS CHARD: 1 pound = 5 to 6 cups packed leaves = 1 to 1½ cups cooked

TOMATOES: 1 pound (3 or 4 medium) = 1½ cups seeded pulp

TURNIPS: 1 pound = 4 cups chopped = 2 cups cooked, mashed

FRUIT EQUIVALENTS

APPLES: 1 pound (3 or 4 medium) = 3 cups sliced

BANANAS: 1 pound (3 or 4 medium) = 1¾ cups mashed

BERRIES: 1 quart = 3½ cups

DATES: 1 pound = 2½ cups pitted

LEMONS: 1 whole = 1 to 3 tablespoons juice; 1 to 1½ teaspoons grated rind

LIMES: 1 whole = 1½ to 2 tablespoons juice

ORANGES: 1 medium = 6 to 8 tablespoons juice; 2 to 3 tablespoons grated rind

PEACHES: 1 pound (4 medium) = 3 cups sliced

PEARS: 1 pound (4 medium) = 2 cups sliced

RHUBARB: 1 pound = 2 cups cooked

REFERENCE

❧ MINIMUM TEMPERATURES FOR MEAT AND POULTRY ❧

WHEN IS IT DONE?

When cooking meat and poultry, interior temperature is a critical factor for safety and for flavor. To be certain of the correct doneness, use an instant-read thermometer, which will give a reading quickly but is not ovenproof and must not be left in the meat while cooking. Use the thermometer toward the end of the minimum cooking time and allow it to remain in the meat for only 15 seconds at a depth of 2 inches, or to the indicator mark on the thermometer's stem. Follow these guidelines for accurate readings:

- For roasts, steaks, and thick chops, insert the thermometer into the center at the thickest part, away from bone, fat, and gristle.
- For whole poultry, insert the thermometer into the inner thigh area near the breast but not touching bone.
- For ground meat (such as meat loaf), insert the thermometer into the thickest area.
- For thin items such as chops and hamburger patties, insert the thermometer sideways.

❧ MINIMUM INTERNAL TEMPERATURES FOR MEAT AND POULTRY ❧

PRODUCT	MINIMUM FAHRENHEIT	PRODUCT	MINIMUM FAHRENHEIT
BEEF (ROASTS, STEAKS, AND CHOPS)		**HAM**	
Rare (some bacterial risk)	140°	Fresh (raw)	160°
Medium	160°	Precooked (to reheat)	140°
Well-done	170°	**LAMB (ROASTS, STEAKS, AND CHOPS)**	
CASSEROLES	160°	Medium-rare	145°
CHICKEN		Medium	160°
Ground	170°	Well-done	170°
Whole	180°	Leftovers	165°
Breasts, roasts	170°	**PORK, FRESH**	
Parts (thighs, wings)	Cook until juices run clear	Medium	160°
DUCK	180°	Well-done	170°
GOOSE	180°	**STUFFING** (cooked alone or in bird)	165°
GRAVIES, SAUCES, AND SOUPS	Bring to a boil	**TURKEY**	
GROUND BEEF, LAMB, PORK, AND VEAL	160°	Ground	170°
		Whole	180°

According to the National Cattlemen's Beef Association, beef roasts can be removed from the oven when the thermometer registers about 5°F below the desired doneness and allowed to stand for about 15 minutes. The outside layers will continue to transfer heat to the center of the roast until it reaches the desired doneness. —courtesy Food Safety and Inspection Service, USDA

❦ INDEX ❧

SPREAD PHOTO CREDITS: 6: Dmytro Gilitukha/Shutterstock. 18: Olena Kaminetska/Shutterstock. 46: Natalia Klenova/Shutterstock.
86: Yuliya Gontar/Shutterstock. 112: Family Business/Shutterstock. 178: Alexey Sun/Shutterstock. 196: Daria Minaeva/Shutterstock.
OUR RECIPE TESTERS: Catherine Boeckmann, Mare-Anne Jarvela, Sherin Pierce, Sarah L. Perreault, Lucille Rines,
Melissa Salo, Cynthia Schlosser, Janice Stillman, Heidi Stonehill, Dariana Travis

INDEX